WHAT HAPPENED
TO TUESDAY?

Thank you'd may God Bless you
beyond measure.

Johanna

WHAT HAPPENED TO TUESDAY?

Shanna McCollum Thomas

Heavenly
Light Press
Alpharetta, Georgia

ISBN: 978-1-6653-0589-1

This ISBN is the property of Heavenly Light Press (a Division of BookLogix) for the express purpose of sales and distribution of this title. The content of this book is the property of the copyright holder only. Heavenly Light Press does not hold any ownership of the content of this book and is not liable in any way for the materials contained within. The views and opinions expressed in this book are the property of the Author/Copyright holder, and do not necessarily reflect those of Heavenly Light Press/BookLogix.

Library of Congress Control Number: 2023906617

Printed in the United States of America

♾This paper meets the requirements of ANSI/NISO Z39.48-1992 (Permanence of Paper)

042023

CONTENTS

Second Quarter

INTRODUCTION

There is nothing like a mother's love. It is forgiving. It is patient. It is kind. It is gentle. It is comforting. It is unbreakable. The strength she endures is like no other. The mother, the matriarch of the family, is the one who keeps the family deeply rooted in spirit and in truth. She carries the weight of the family in times of need, and she never seems to have a visible breaking point. This was true of my granny, the late Pinkie Bell Wright, and it is certainly true of my mother, Evelyn Wright Dunham.

My granny always told me to do right by people, family included, even if they do you wrong. Love everyone, but you do not have to like their ways. Talk to God in prayer and seek all understanding.

My mother, Evelyn, who is wise in her own right, always told me to put God first in everything and wait on the Lord; your attitude will determine your altitude in life, and patience is a virtue.

I always struggled with that patience part—*and still do.* God chose me to be a part of this lineage of strong mothers. No matter what tore us apart as a family, when we needed one another, nothing else mattered and all was forgotten; at least for the moment, but that's the *Gemini* in me. But I digress.

The matriarch of my family, my mother, is affectionately known as "Grandma" to all. She is a retired media specialist of 36 years. After she retired, she continued to substitute for another eight years. Then she moved to Acworth, Georgia, to be closer to us. She is a feisty and fiery golden-ager who is active in the church. She loves to travel and is very talkative but accuses everyone else of talking too much. She is the peacemaker of the family.

My husband is a chef and has worked in various kitchens, from five-star restaurants to clubs to mom-and-pop restaurants to our own family business, Team Thomas Catering, LLC. He is a family man and has a strong affinity for all children. He loves me unconditionally, and the bond between my mother and him is so close that most think he's her son and I'm her daughter-in-law. He still thinks he's young, athletically, until he wakes up the next day. His stories of us and how we grew up remind me of Heathcliff Huxtable, the father from *The Cosby Show,* because they are so colorful. But I wouldn't trade him in for the world.

As for me, I'm a licensed chiropractor, approaching my 17th year of practicing. I've practiced in the states of New York and Georgia in personal injury clinics and in wellness clinics. For the past eight years, I have been with a nationwide chiropractic franchise. With my big personality and infectious smile, no one is a stranger. I'll talk to any and everyone. People are naturally drawn to me, and I love every minute of it. I'm so intrigued by their story and what makes them who they are.

My husband and I met over 32 years ago. My church choir was the guest choir at his church. He made it known that I was cute, and three years later, we were courting. We'd dated off and on since 1994. By 2004, we committed to each other and married on December 24, 2007. Our wedding was unforgettable. We were married at the courthouse. Our wedding party consisted of another newlywed couple, a Caucasian man and an Asian lady, and about 20 of her Asian family members. This Caucasian judge walked in, looked at this Black couple, Caucasian guy, and several Asians, and asked if he was in the right room as his face turned red as ever. We laughed, and the rest is history.

Out of this union are our three daughters and one son. Camryn is our oldest daughter. She's our creative child. She only paints on blank canvases, draws free hand, taught herself how to play the piano, loves all genres of music and musicals, and although she is low-key about singing, she really can sing. She's the quiet one of the family, stays to herself, and thinks everything we do is embarrassing.

Kendall is our second-oldest daughter. Kendall is the social butterfly. She has a giving spirit, is loveable, and knows everybody.

She's a hard worker and very passionate about football. She has always danced to her own beat and always thought outside of the box. Hence, the only female on the North Paulding High School freshman football team. By the way, she played football in fifth grade as well. When the coach asked Kendall if she wanted to play *flag football*, Kendall said, "No, because they don't tackle." And from that point, the coach knew he was not dealing with just *any* girl.

Chase is the only boy and third-born. He's the sweetheart of the family. He's a lover and not a fighter. He's passionate and loves sports, especially football and basketball. He's a giver and wants to help every homeless person he sees. He always has a smile on his face.

Finally, there's Kaiden, who is our youngest daughter. She is the drama queen and is a whole movement by herself. To know her is to love her. She's sassy, sweet, smart, outgoing, and a true boss baby. She will argue with you until you tap out.

Together, we are Team Thomas. We move as a unit when it comes to traveling, eating, playing, and praying. We even coordinate our wardrobes most Sundays. We're a comedy show in the making, and our personalities together are the perfect ingredients to get us through this recipe we call life. We are a team, not because of our quantity but because our togetherness is our happy place. We are Team Thomas, party of seven, and nothing can break us.

This is the story of Team Thomas and how the actions of one person had a piercing and life-altering effect on my family. It was the unimaginable tragedy and near fatality of my daughter, Kendall Elise Thomas, who will later become the epitome of the power of prayer.

FIRST QUARTER

ONE

The Unimaginable Call

⤙⤙⤙⤙⤙✝⤚⤚⤚⤚⤚

January 11

It's 2022, and I thought we would have been over this pandemic by now. We've been trying to process living before, during, and after COVID. At this point, my husband, my son, and myself had our bout with COVID over the past two years. I believe my mother had COVID before we knew it was a thing. She was sick for the month of January in 2020 after we returned from our seven-day Christmas cruise to Belize, the Cayman Islands, Honduras, and Cozumel.

I'm currently dealing with my second round of COVID and have been in quarantine for five days. I have lost my sense of taste, have a sore throat, and a burning sensation in my nose. Other than that, I feel much better this time around than my first encounter with COVID.

Today feels no different than any other day in quarantine. My mother and my husband were up early with the kids, getting them off to school, sharing their words of wisdom and saying their "I love yous." My husband, as usual, prepared and cooked all my meals, including creating these nasty concoctions—I mean, home remedies—to help me battle my COVID symptoms. To pass my time along, I had been binge-watching this series entitled *Money Heist*.

It was approaching time for Kaiden to get home from school, and in her clockwork-like fashion, she called me on the phone at

3:08 p.m. to tell me all about her day. We talked and laughed, and then she said, "You know, I'm going to call you back soon." Of course she was, because every weekday around 4:00 p.m., she calls me and inquires about what snack should she have.

It was 3:58 p.m. The phone rings. I answer, and it's Kaiden as expected. But what she said next was the unexpected. Her voice was trembling; she spoke to me with a screeching, crying tone. "Mama, Mama, call Daddy. Kendall was in an accident! Call Daddy! Mama, call Daddy! Hang up. Call Daddy!"

As she's speaking to me with a sense of urgency, I hastily got up from my recliner in my retreat area and looked out of our bathroom window. My husband's truck was gone, and I began to panic. I called my husband. No answer. I called my mama. No answer. I called my husband back. No answer. I called my mama. She finally answered.

As much as she tried to disguise her knowledge of Kendall's accident, my mama broke down and told me that it was true. I hung up and called my husband again. He answers as he is flying to the school to get to Kendall. All he knew was Kendall was hit and a bus was involved. Immediately, horrific images flashed in my mind, and I couldn't stop crying because of the "hows" and the "whys."

I kept receiving calls from the mother of one of Chase's teammates. She called me over and over, but I didn't answer. I finally answered. She told me she witnessed Kendall's accident and asked if there was anything she could do for me. She said she could bring Chase home, but by that time, that part was taken care of.

As I began to cry aloud, I said, "Please tell me what happened!"

She said, "Shanna, please ask me anything but that. Please don't ask me."

I begged, pleaded, screamed, and cried out to God. I continued to ask her, "Please tell me. That's what you can do!"

She began to cry more with a shaking voice and said, "Shanna, it's bad. It's bad."

I screamed louder and louder, kept swaying from side to side, shaking my head, and high-stepping very slowly in a twisted motion. My hands began to sweat, and my stomach was in knots as she began to tell me what happened to my daughter, Kendall.

She said Kendall was waiting at the crosswalk as buses were passing. A school bus stopped, and Kendall proceeded to cross. Kendall was almost to the other side of the street when a vehicle struck her. Kendall's body flew up, and she landed on the left side of her head.

I hollered and dropped my phone. I couldn't see. I couldn't hear. I couldn't think. All I knew was, COVID or not, I had to get to my baby girl. I immediately called my husband and shared with him what I was told. He was driving frantically behind the ambulance as they were headed to Kennestone Hospital in Marietta, Georgia.

I hung up with him and waited for his call once he arrived at the hospital, but my broken soul wouldn't allow me to sit still. I called some of everybody, searching for comfort, understanding, and peace. But no one was giving me the satisfaction I needed to ease my broken heart and my disturbed mind. I got dressed, masked up, and fought my way past my mother, my sister, and a sistafriend of mine. They gave up trying to hold me down, and my sister hesitantly drove me to the hospital.

With me having COVID, I was outside in the dead of winter, pacing back and forth, crying, praying, screaming, rubbing my head, trying to process how we got here. I mean, Kendall and I were just joking over the phone about the Georgia vs. Alabama game. She's a die-hard Bulldog fan, and I'm Alabama all day. I just told her I loved her as she headed to bed. Out of all the calls I anticipated with her playing football, this is the one call that was unexpected. This can't be real. This is the day that time stood still.

Kendall had to have emergency brain surgery on the right side. Her skull had to be removed due to the swelling of her brain. Her neurosurgeon spoke with us briefly because Kendall required a second emergency brain surgery on the left side. After six hours of surgery, with me wearing out the cement in the parking deck, Kendall was finally taken to the neuro ICU.

The athletic director, Kendall's coach, our executive pastor, my sister, my sistafriend, our cousin, my husband, and I prayed. My husband held me tight and kissed me on my forehead. He had to stay with Kendall, and the rest of us departed. The mood was eerie, and the ride home was a blur.

Before I lay down to only stare at the top of the canopy on my bed, my husband texted me a photo of Kendall. There she was, lying motionless and dressed in a navy-blue hospital gown, with wires, tubes, and drains going into her from head to toe. She was on a ventilator and connected to a coolant machine to help maintain her core body temperature and a monitor to measure her heart rate, blood pressure, brain pressure, and oxygen levels. Her face and lips were swollen, and her eyes and hands were closed tightly.

This wasn't my Kendall. Lord, help me!

TWO

THE CHASE

☙☙☙☙☙✝☙☙☙☙☙

January 12

Can't sleep. Won't eat. My phone is ringing and vibrating non-stop, but I just can't respond. It's too much. So many versions of Kendall's accident are flooding my ears, and the news media outlets are lining up for interviews. This time yesterday, my life was good. Kendall was just a girl headed to football practice for speed and agility training, and I was just counting down the days left in quarantine. If I could just turn back the hands of time.

I was in agony. I couldn't be there for any of my children or seek comfort in my mother's arms or lean on my husband when I needed him the most. To make matters worse, my husband and I just found out that our son, Chase, witnessed Kendall's accident.

Chase plays football as well but for the sixth-grade team. In the off-season, the middle and high schoolers train together. They walk up to the high school and wait outside until the high schoolers are dismissed; student drivers, buses, and walkers leave at the same time. Chaos on top of chaos.

When Kendall was struck, she landed right in front of her brother. Immediately after the accident, Kendall's coach gathered students and began to talk to them about what they witnessed. As the coach panned the crowd, he noticed Chase was among the crowd with tears flowing from his face uncontrollably. He quickly grabbed him and called me.

The hardest part of this day was the chase. I was chasing answers,

7

chasing comfort, chasing hope, chasing my pain away, and chasing Chase; but it was a race that was impossible to win. I tried to distract myself with social media, but it was an epic failure.

My social media memory was pictures of the late Rev. Dr. Kenneth E. Marcus, my beloved pastor of almost eighteen years. Today was the anniversary of his death, four years ago. The bond we had with him was impeccable. He was a man of honor and distinction; his soul and his demeanor were so captivating. I would have given anything to hear his words of wisdom and comfort. I'm chasing a memory of what was and what could have been. The chase . . .

Meanwhile, Kendall was facing the chase of her life. The left side of her skull was fractured, and her brain was swollen with deep bruising. No other fractures, including her spine and chest, were detected. She developed pneumonia, which is common with traumatic brain injuries.

Kendall is still unconscious, but no further brain scans were necessary. Team Thomas is surviving off of the many prayers being lifted during this difficult time. The outpouring of love is remarkable.

THREE

UNCONSCIOUSLY CONSCIOUS

చాచాచాచాచా✝చాచాచాచాచా

January 13

Today is Founder's Day for the ladies of Delta Sigma Theta Sorority, Inc., my sorority, and I should be painting the city red with my line sisters. But my head is spinning out of control, my body is weak, and my soul is broken.

It's been three days since I've seen Kendall or heard her voice. Three days of my life that quickly spiraled down. Three days of separation from my husband who needs me just as much as I need him because we're living in two separate hells right now. It pains me to even talk to him. All I hear is the unbearable hurt in his voice, and I see the hopelessness on his face.

I'm here but I'm not present; somehow, I'm unconsciously conscious. I can't feel anything. I can't see anything. I can't move anything. But I am aware of my surroundings. I'm unconsciously conscious. My mind is inaccessible, but my emotions are untamed. I'm unconsciously conscious.

Kendall is still unconscious and has little reaction to light, but she is stABLE and God is ABLE. Keep praying. She feels them . . . we need them.

Kendall is stABLE and God is ABLE.

FOUR

P. U. S. H. FOR KENDALL

꙳꙳꙳꙳꙳✝꙳꙳꙳꙳꙳

January 14

I've always gone to God in prayer, but I never knew the magnitude of prayer until January 11, 2022. Prior to that, my prayers were generally selfish. I wanted God to move on my time. I wanted God to put my prayer requests at the top because I didn't know how to wait on the Lord. When things didn't turn out how I expected them to, then I went to God more frequently.

I was raised in the church. As a child, I went to Sunday School, all-day church, everybody's Vacation Bible School (VBS), Bible study, pastor's aide meetings, missionary meetings, stewardess meetings, usher board meetings, sang in the choir, and played for the children's choir. You name it, I *had* to do it. I was churching before I knew what church was all about.

My husband was raised the same way, and we instilled those same values in our own children. So why wouldn't God hear and answer *my* prayers? But the problem was, I was talking *at* God and not talking *to* God. I was in and at the church, but I wasn't the church outside of church. I didn't talk to God daily. I didn't know the power of prayer for myself.

All this time, the prayers of my mother, grandmother, and my ancestors were the prayers that were sustaining me. As much as I need God to move right now for Kendall's sake and my sanity, I don't even have enough strength to muster up a prayer. All I keep doing is crying out to God, but what I didn't realize was that my crying out was a prayer.

After I have done all that I can, all I can do is just stand still. And when I look down and notice only one set of footprints, I know God is carrying me.

Now, I P. U. S. H. for Kendall. *Pray Until Something Happens* for Kendall. *Pray Until Something Happens* for Team Thomas. *Pray Until Something Happens* for the entire community.

My husband shared a picture of Kendall with me. She was wrapped in a prayer blanket given to her by one of the chaplains at Kennestone Hospital. Although she is still unconscious with a swollen brain and elevated blood pressure, she looks at peace. That was God's way of telling me to keep pushing.

Kendall is stABLE and God is ABLE.

FIVE

MAMA IS HERE

☙☙☙☙☙✝❧❧❧❧❧

January 15

Everything I had longed for during the last few days of my quarantine was finally granted. I was COVID-free. I desperately needed to be smothered in love by my family. Kendall needed to feel my presence, and I needed to be in hers.

Although I was eager to see Kendall, I was very apprehensive as I packed my suitcase. This would be the first time I wasn't living through my husband's eyes. I would see Kendall in person, with several apparatuses connected to her. I would see her in the flesh, motionless, yet fighting for her life. I would see the fear, anger, and hurt in my husband's face and not the obscured version of him through a video call. The beeps and alarms of the medical equipment would no longer be muffled—they would be loud and clear.

The closer we got to the hospital, the more my tears fell. I couldn't stop them. I was trying to pull it together because I didn't want Kendall to feel this type of energy from me—only positive vibes. My mind was wandering, my tears were trying to dry up, my heart was pounding, my stomach felt uneasy, and my limbs were feeble. I kept telling myself, *Don't break, keep it together. You can do this; this is what you wanted. You are who she needs.*

I opened the door expecting the worst-possible sight. But God knew exactly what I needed to see—Kendall wrapped in her prayer blanket. For a moment, the room was silent. The atmosphere had a calmness about it, and I felt like a heavy weight had been lifted. I held her hand, leaned over, and whispered in her ear, "Mama is here. Whenever you feel someone gently rub your nose, just know that it is me. Mama is here."

Kendall is stABLE and God is ABLE.

SIX

TODAY IS A GOOD DAY

༄༅ ༄ ༄ ༄ ✝ ᭫ ᭫ ᭫ ᭫ ᭫

January 16

The last two days have been good for Kendall. Her lab readings are normal. She's on minimal ventilation. Prayerfully, within a week or so, she will have the breathing tube removed and get a tracheostomy tube; this will help decrease her risk of infection. There has been no bleeding on the right side of her brain in the last 48 hours, so that drain will be removed; two more drains to go!

Kendall has also been moving her arms. At this point in her recovery, her neurosurgeon is not certain if it's purposeful or involuntary. It could be both, but any movement is good.

This road to recovery is a marathon, not a sprint. I know every day won't be a good day because bad days will come. Kendall may be unconscious, but she is fighting. She is still here, and we are still standing because of your prayers.

I don't know the why yet, but God is giving us the peace we need in the midst of our storm. All we can do is give Him all the praise, only looking to Him because today is a Good Day.

Kendall is stABLE and God is ABLE.

SEVEN

THE STORMS OF LIFE

❧❧❧❧❧✝❧❧❧❧❧

January 17

We were awakened to the sounds of feet shuffling, alarms going haywire, and Kendall's neuro team chattering with a sense of urgency in tone. Kendall was shivering rapidly. Her heart rate spiked, her blood pressure elevated, she had a high fever, and her arms were involuntarily moving unrhythmically. Her stomach was hard and swollen, which was not allowing the passage of any fluid or food. This eventually led to her projectile vomiting. This was the start of Kendall's neurostorming. All the doctors could do was adjust her medications and/or try new ones.

I couldn't get these horrifying thoughts out of my head. *Is this the day we have to say goodbye? Is this the second day I'm going to hate? Is this the day all hope is lost, never to return? Is this the day my shattered heart will never be mendable?*

This thunderstorm in my life is overwhelming, and there's no shelter in sight. My visibility is hazy, and the raging waters of life are pulling me under. Just as I was engulfed in my thoughts, the neurostorming started to cease. Kendall's vitals were stabilizing, and her body stopped the unrhythmic movement.

At this point in her care, it was a watch and see; and at this point in our life, our faith was watch and see. God never gives us more than we can bear.

Kendall is stABLE and God is ABLE.

EIGHT

43 SECONDS

🍃🍃🍃🍃🍃✝🍃🍃🍃🍃🍃

January 18

Exactly one week ago, our world was turned upside down. We received a call that our daughter, Kendall Elise Thomas, age 14, was struck by a vehicle at school and was unconscious.

Kendall's body collided with the front end of a vehicle. She flew upward only to land on her head, just a few feet in front of her younger brother, Chase.

I still can't grasp how such a senseless act could happen. School should be a safe haven. Crossing the street in a crosswalk should be a safe haven. The adults on duty should be able to keep the children safe. But where was Kendall's safety net?

This unimaginable and terrifying accident not only affected the two families involved, but it caused a ripple effect of devastation across the entire community.

I am angry. I am furious. I am brokenhearted. I am at a loss.

Kendall was the only female player on the North Paulding High School freshman football team. She was the nose guard, and her number was 43. She originally wanted the number 15 because that's the day she was born. Unfortunately, it was already taken. Then she chose 43 because that's how old I was. She said I was her biggest cheerleader and advocate for playing football.

Her high school basketball team, as well as other high school teams around the surrounding counties, started taking a moment of silence for 43 seconds before every game. When two or more are gathered in His name, God is present.

Every Tuesday, around 3:50 p.m., I started soliciting prayers or a 43-second moment of silence. I believe if we bombard heaven with prayers on behalf of Kendall at the same time, God will move mountains and do the impossible.

Kendall is stABLE and God is ABLE.

NINE

The Power of Prayer

ঔঔঔঔঔ✝ঔঔঔঔঔ

January 19

Yesterday at 3:50 p.m., prayers all over the world, including the US, Canada, Jamaica, and Africa, were being said for Kendall.

As my husband and I were preparing to pray ourselves, the doctor walked into the room at 3:48 p.m. The critical-care doctor was informing us of Kendall's next steps and reassuring us that she is getting the best care. Then, the doctor left.

My husband and I were both holding Kendall's hand, praying and talking to her. I noticed her mouth needed to be wiped. As I wiped her mouth, she squeezed both our hands! HALLELUJAH! I don't know if it's her or a neurological response, but what I do know is that God gave us something we needed right on (His) time.

Yesterday was one of our roughest days mentally. We were broken, hurting, crying, having bad thoughts, unfocused, not eating, and exhausted. BUT GOD . . . BUT GOD . . .

We are asking for those same powerful prayers that have carried us thus far to keep coming. Kendall has three procedures tentatively scheduled for today to help put her in a better recovery state. She is getting a bronchoscopy, as we speak, to clear her lungs from mucus buildup. And later today, prayerfully, they will remove the ventilator and insert a tracheostomy tube and a feeding tube.

Kendall is stABLE and God is ABLE.

TEN

NEUROSTORMS

೮ೆ೮ೆ೮ೆ೮ೆ೮ೆ✝೮ೆ೮ೆ೮ೆ೮ೆ೮ೆ

January 20

Kendall had a successful bronchoscopy yesterday. However, the tracheostomy and feeding tube are being delayed for further clearance. Prayerfully, those procedures will take place this weekend or early next week.

Kendall has been neurostorming, and her stats have dropped twice. They are stabilizing her with various medications; praying that this cocktail will work. The neurosurgeon did remove the drain on the left side of her brain, and the stitches above her left eye were removed as well.

Three days have passed, and Kendall is still neurostorming (spike in heart rate and blood pressure, fever, vigorous shivering, and a decrease in oxygen) several times this weekend. Although this is common for traumatic brain injuries, the goal is to find the right medication combination to keep her from having them. Currently, her brain is just sending all kinds of signals, which means the cocktails (medicine combinations) that stopped her neurostorming previously are not working anymore. This is a constant problem at this phase in her recovery; what may work one minute may not work the next.

Although Kendall is neurostorming sporadically, the electrodes from her brain have been removed because she has not had any seizures. She also has been cleared to have the tracheostomy and feeding tube. All we can do is just pray and hold tight to each other. We're still in this marathon together.

Kendall is stABLE and God is ABLE.

ELEVEN

PROMISE KEEPER

⌘⌘⌘⌘⌘†⌘⌘⌘⌘⌘

January 24

Kendall had two successful surgeries this morning—the tracheostomy tube and the feeding tube. Although she is heavily sedated, she is comfortable.

We are so thankful and grateful for this marathon we're in—for the good and the bad days. Your prayers are with us always in our darkest moments, carrying us when we are weak and uplifting us right on time. And for that, WE ARE BLESSED.

My emotions are all over the place, and I am struggling to block outside voices. Everyone is in our ear regarding attorneys and what is happening to the person that struck Kendall. Others are still questioning her diagnosis, her prognosis, and her place of care. Some are even wondering if we are going back to work. Right now, my only concern is Kendall.

I still don't know where this journey is taking us or exactly what my purpose is in life. I don't know the outcome of Kendall's situation. I don't know how long this journey will be. I don't know whether I'm coming or going most days. But I do know that with God, anything is possible. I know He is a promise keeper. I know He is a way-maker. I know He is my light in the darkness. I know He will never leave me.

Kendall is stABLE and God is ABLE.

TWELVE

A WORLDWIDE
PRAYER FOR KENDALL

෨෨෨෨෨෨†෨෨෨෨෨෨

January 25

It's been two weeks to the day when a major shift occurred in our lives. Our 14-year-old daughter, Kendall, was in a horrific accident at school. I still can't wrap my head around the fact that she was struck while in a crosswalk. I still can't wrap my head around the fact that she landed on her head in front of her 11-year-old brother, Chase. I still can't wrap my head around the fact that so many witnessed this tragedy and there is nothing I can do. There is nothing anyone can say or do to erase this day and erase the emptiness in my heart.

For the past two weeks, my husband and I have watched Kendall fight for her life. We have seen her look from lifeless and motionless to moving uncontrollably and vigorously. We have seen her stats on this merry-go-round of stability and plummeting. Yet somehow, we can see her fight and feel her presence. Somehow, we can keep fighting for her and with her, regardless of our emotional state and what we witness hour by hour.

We are trusting and believing in God and in His miraculous, healing powers. We are learning to lean on others for support. We are adjusting to hospital living. We are trying to figure out how to be here for Kendall as well as our other three children who are home with my mother. We are preparing to weather this storm.

We are attempting to manage our stress. We are making a conscious effort not to break.

Kendall's near fatality occurred around 3:50 p.m. Every Tuesday at 3:50 p.m., we will come together in prayer or take a moment of silence for 43 seconds. These prayers will uplift us. These prayers will move mountains. These prayers will be spoken on Kendall's behalf. These prayers will carry us through.

Kendall is stABLE and God is ABLE.

THIRTEEN

THE WEANING PROCESS

❧❧❧❧❧✝❧❧❧❧❧

January 27

The critical care team has been weening Kendall off one of the opioids. This will help her become more conscious—in other words, give her the ability to wake up. The downfall of it is that it will also cause her to neurostorm more frequently. The less sedated she is, the more easily she is stimulated, which unfortunately causes her to neurostorm.

Kendall has been constantly neurostorming since she has been weaning off one of her medications. It's been challenging to figure out the right medicine combination to keep her heart rate and blood pressure stable without neurostorming. Every time another medication is being weaned, another round of neurostorming will occur. This will be an ongoing battle until she is completely off all of her invasive IV medications. By the way, there are eight of them. Remember, we are in a marathon.

In the midst of her neurostorming, small victories are still being won. Her third and final drain, which was inside her brain, was removed yesterday. That drain measured her brain pressure and removed fluid her brain could not absorb. She is now at a point in her recovery in which her brain can absorb its own fluid (cerebral spinal fluid). She will still be monitored closely, and if anything changes with her neurologically, the drain will have to be put back.

Every second of every day, Kendall's brain is constantly changing.

Her stats are consistently alternating between steady and plunging. And like Kendall's body, my mental state is constantly fluctuating as well. But one thing that is persistent is the prayers.

Kendall is stABLE and God is ABLE.

FOURTEEN

MIRACLE WORKER

ᡃᡃᡃᡃᡃ✝ᡃᡃᡃᡃᡃ

January 29

My husband and I have finally figured out a schedule to help balance our home and hospital lifestyle. We decided to split our time: one of us will stay at the hospital with Kendall, and the other one will go home for a three-day period. This allows our other children to see at least one of us every day. It also allows us to experience life again outside of these hospital walls. It gives us a sense of normalcy. We also video conference each other when any doctor comes into Kendall's room. That way, the information is not butchered or misinterpreted.

It was my turn to be home. I was embracing every moment, taking extended hot showers, sleeping in my bed, and eating home-cooked meals. I was in temporary mama mode with the kids; my mama had me in full chauffeur mode with her as I drove her all over Acworth and Marietta. For a moment, it was like old times.

As my mother and I were driving to our next venture, my phone began ringing nonstop, and my notifications from social media were chiming. Before I could check anything, my husband called me and said Kendall opened her eyes. I was filled with mixed emotions. On one hand, I was excited, but on the other hand, I was sad because I wasn't there. My husband sent me a picture and the tears started flowing as the praises were going up.

My husband was so excited that he posted it on social media, and everyone thought Kendall was conscious and had finally awakened. Unfortunately, this was not the case.

Although she is still unconscious, her left eye opening is GOoD news! She has also been responding to light stimuli during her neurological examinations. Her next set of goals will be to wean her off oxygen to see if she can breathe on her own as well as find the right medicine combination. She never needed a ventilator; however, for any traumatic brain injury, the standard protocol is to vent. Machines have been breathing for her for three weeks. This weakens her lungs and, therefore, her lungs must be retrained.

God is truly a miracle worker. There have been so many moments when I thought I would never see Kendall's eyes open. There have been so many times when I thought it was over. There have been so many times I could have easily given up. But thank God for His miraculous power. We still have a long way to go. Every little step in a positive direction is a mighty victory.

Kendall is stABLE and God is ABLE.

FIFTEEN

PRAYING FOR A LIGHT IN THE DARKNESS

ﾐ⧽ﾐ⧽ﾐ⧽ﾐ⧽ﾐ⧽†ﾐ⧼ﾐ⧼ﾐ⧼ﾐ⧼ﾐ⧼

February 1

My husband and I finally looked at the police report for the first time. We now know the exact time EMS was called, when they arrived at the scene, when they arrived at the hospital, and everything else that is on a police report. That took us right back to that unfortunate moment three weeks ago.

Yesterday was tough on us mentally because of all of the hard conversations we had to have. Then the night before, Kendall had a setback. Opening her eyes was just for a brief moment. She was neurostorming off and on for most of the day. It was so bad they thought she was having seizures. Her oxygen levels dropped drastically. Fevers spiked. So, they had to increase her oxygen, increase her strong medications back to the Day One dosage, and alter her other ones. The leads were placed back on her head to measure seizure activity . . . this is that MARATHON.

Today at 3:38 p.m. (the time EMS was called), we are asking everyone to pray for everyone directly involved in this tragedy and their families. Pray for peace, comfort, healing, and the mental state of both families affected, for my husband and I to be able to make the right decisions, for Kendall to wake up, for Kendall's brain to function properly—no more neurostorming—the right medicine combination, and for Kendall's entire medical team.

Kendall is stABLE and God is ABLE.

SIXTEEN

THE POWER OF GOD AND YOUR PRAYERS

✿✿✿✿✿✿✿✝✿✿✿✿✿✿

February 4

On Tuesday, I asked y'all to pray for specific things and all I can say is MY GOD . . . BUT GOD . . . prayer changes things.

Kendall has been stable for the past four days. The doctors have been weaning her slowly off of her strong medications as well as her blood pressure medication.

The respiratory team placed her ventilator on pressure ventilation for six hours a day. Pressure ventilation is when each breath is initiated by the patient but is supported by constant pressure inflation. This means Kendall is breathing on her own and if or when she stops, the ventilator will be activated.

For three days, she has not had any breathing episodes and has only had one mild episode of neurostorming. She is on the lowest dosage for her blood pressure medication.

There is a GOD, and He knows, hears, and answers our prayers.

Kendall is stABLE and God is ABLE.

SEVENTEEN

WEEPING MAY ENDURE FOR A NIGHT, BUT JOY COMES IN THE MORNING

꩜꩜꩜꩜꩜✝꩜꩜꩜꩜꩜

February 8

Psalm 30:5 has always had me believing that after one bad night, the next day would be better. Clearly, I was wrong. This scripture has taken on a new meaning since January 11, 2022. It is a display of God's timing. A night could mean days, weeks, months, or years, but JOY will come.

It's Week Four . . . Four weeks of Kendall being unconscious; four weeks of Kendall neurostorming off and on (with this past weekend being the scariest events of neurostorming); four weeks of her neuro team doing the best that they can every minute of the day; four weeks of trying so hard not to fall apart, that we fall apart; four weeks of trying to figure out how to answer two questions that were so easy to answer four weeks ago: *How are you? Is there anything you need?*

It's been four weeks of trying to balance hospital and home life and maintain some sense of normalcy; four weeks of realizing that what we thought was important or a must-have is really not.

But we have also had four weeks of prayers from across the world; four weeks of blessings in all forms; four weeks of God's favor; four weeks of incredible strength that only comes from God.

Kendall had a rough weekend. Her neurostorming was the scariest ordeal we've had to face so far. Her fevers wouldn't break, her oxygen levels kept dropping, her heart rate was high, and she was shaking so bad, as if she were having seizures. She was like this from Friday night until Sunday evening. Neurostorming is the hardest to control and is the worst in young people because they are still developing.

Kendall is also battling some type of infection, but all of her tests so far have been negative. We are waiting on more results from other diagnostic testing. She will also have a lumbar puncture this morning to test her spinal/brain fluid. Kendall's eyes are opening more, but it's not purposeful.

Kendall is stABLE and God is ABLE.

EIGHTEEN

Searching for the Calm

✿✿✿✿✿†✿✿✿✿✿

February 12

There is always a calm before the storm, and after the raging waters, there is a stillness.

We are facing the biggest storm of our lives, but we know that a calming of the sea will come. Kendall is still unconscious. She is not in a medically induced coma; she's just not awakened from the accident.

She is battling with infections from two different bacteria. She also has a blood clot in her pelvis. She's been vomiting and coughing more frequently, which alters her breathing. She neurostorms off and on.

Through it all, she is still able to tolerate some weaning of certain medications and maintain a low-grade fever instead of the 102 and 103 fevers. She is a true fighter.

Weeping may come . . . BUT JOY . . . BUT GOD.

Kendall is stABLE and God is ABLE.

NINETEEN

WHAT IS LOVE?

࿔࿔࿔࿔࿔✝࿔࿔࿔࿔࿔

February 15

A very near and dear sistafriend of mine sent me a message yesterday that came right on time. She stumbled across a passage that says, "To love is to extend oneself for the spiritual growth of themselves or another." She said that when I find myself wanting to question God (normal), think of this kind of love.

When I am in despair, I ask myself, "What are God and our ancestors teaching me? What do they want me to know?"

She believes what I am (we are) going through right now is both of these kinds of love.

Shortly after I received this message, the mother of the young lady that struck Kendall exactly five weeks ago messaged me. When I saw her name, my heart sank. I knew exactly who she was without hesitation. My emotions were getting the best of me. I was beginning to have the wrong thoughts in my head. So, I waited . . .

It took a supernatural power to read her message. I won't disclose the details because I'm quite sure it took that same supernatural power for her to even reach out to me. My ability not to react, and her strength to reach out, is that spiritual growth, that type of love my sistafriend spoke of.

Our focus is only on Kendall.

Not much has changed with Kendall. She's still unconscious. She's still battling her infections, vomiting, and neurostorming off and on. She's easily stimulated, which is good, but sometimes it causes her to neurostorm. Her fevers seem to be getting under control. The swelling of the brain is decreasing.

They are weaning her off medications even slower than before. This will help her transition better from IV medications to pill form—one of the most important requirements in order for her to start inpatient rehabilitation.

Kendall's road to recovery is a MARATHON. We are only in the WARM-UP phase of this race.

What Love Is . . .

People coming together, standing in the gap for Team Thomas, not only on TUESDAYS but every day, PRAYING. People who we don't know, people who had no faith, people who had little faith, people who see our faith, people who hurt for/with us, people who don't usually pray, people who are dealing with their own battles . . . ARE PRAYING. THIS IS LOVE. Love endures.

Kendall is stABLE and God is ABLE.

TWENTY

When Praises Go Up

☙☙☙☙☙✝☙☙☙☙☙

February 22

This past Sunday was our first time going back to church since Kendall's unfortunate accident. We were so apprehensive as a family because we were a team of six instead of seven. We didn't want "the looks," and we didn't want the long hugs . . . we just wanted to be "normal."

When my pastor, Rev. Dr. Taruway Richard Allen Bright, called us to the front to be recognized, my nervousness got the best of me, all of us. My husband, who was the strong one—so I thought—broke down as he was speaking and suddenly passed the microphone to me.

For once, I was speechless, because my husband and I had agreed he would address the church. I paused. Then God gave me strength and the exact words to say. I referenced a movie that was filmed at our church, Turner Chapel AME, about five or six years ago called *A Question of Faith*. It is a movie that centers around three families who are faced with tragedy. Their destiny compels them to travel a path to perceive God's Love, Grace, and Mercy as they face challenges that could restore their faith. Please watch it when you get a chance.

During that film, we were extras, and now we find ourselves being the stars of that film. But our faith is not questioned, and the outcome will be different . . . We had a GOoD cry.

They prayed for us, and all of our anxiety was lifted. A family of six became a family of hundreds. The looks were of empathy. The hugs were comforting. And we felt a sense of normalcy for once.

Blessings come down.

Although Kendall is still unconscious, she has slowly but surely been making progress. Kendall is almost done with her antibiotics, which means the infections are subsiding. She has had two fevers and only one neurostorming episode in the past week. The swelling in her brain is still decreasing. Even though she can't see yet or focus, when you call her name, she opens her eyes. I accidentally dropped the remote and it startled her, which means she can hear.

She is one step closer to getting off of *all* IV medications. She is on the lowest setting of the ventilator and has done well with the test trials of breathing on her own with very few setbacks. She even tolerated the bed being in a chair position for two hours yesterday.

We're still in the WARM-UP phase of this MARATHON. The continuous prayers and the outpouring of love and support are immeasurable.

Kendall is stABLE and God is ABLE.

TWENTY-ONE

COME THROUGH JESUS

༺༺༺༺༺✝༺༺༺༺༺

February 27

Today is Kendall's first time sitting in the cardiac chair. This allows her airways to open more, which helps strengthen her lungs and helps her to breathe more on her own, using less supported oxygen. Although she is dealing with mild neurostorming (low-grade fevers, sweating profusely, increased heart rate, and increased blood pressure), she continues to progress with tolerating smaller tracheostomy tubes and the weaning of some medications.

She is keeping her eyes open longer, although her visual attention is not yet purposeful. Her labs currently show no more signs of infections.

The selfless acts of kindness, love, support, and continuous prayers are being felt. May God's blessing be endless and beyond belief.

Kendall is stABLE and God is ABLE.

TWENTY-TWO

EXPERIENCING
THE UNEXPECTED

෨෨෨෨෨෨✝෨෨෨෨෨෨

March 1

Every Tuesday for the past seven weeks, I have solicited prayers mostly for Kendall. But today, my husband and I need prayer more than ever. Through this whole experience, we have faced some challenging times, difficult moments, and scary situations no parent should ever have to deal with. But yesterday, we received a call informing us of an unexpected harsh reality we will be facing *way* before we intended.

Just when I thought we were getting a handle on our temporary "new normal," God said, "Keep that same faith and strength, because I'm about to put you through a bigger storm, and you will come out even stronger."

We're praying that our anxiety will cease. We're praying that we will make the right decisions regarding Kendall's next phase of care. We're praying that our pride won't get in the way when it comes to leaning on others for help. We're praying that we suppress our anger and put that energy toward Kendall. We're praying that we are able to find a new way to balance caring for our other three children and still be able to be there for Kendall around the clock. We're praying for peace and understanding. We're praying for US.

God orders our steps, and right now, His footsteps are the only ones in the sand because they are carrying us through this. *And through all of this, we can still smile.*

Kendall is still unconscious and neurostorming. She's dealing with fevers, sweating, increased heart rate, and increased blood pressure. Continue to pray for Kendall.

Kendall is stABLE and God is ABLE.

TWENTY-THREE

JESUS, HE KNOWS HOW MUCH WE CAN BEAR

❧❧❧❧❧✝❧❧❧❧❧

March 3

It was our understanding that once Kendall was off all IV med-ication and the ventilator, she would be transferred to a long-term care facility for rehabilitation. Our stay would be similar to what it is now.

My husband and I were planning to go back to work, part-time, just to have some income in the house once Kendall was settled in a rehabilitation facility and we had our routine in place. In our heads, Kendall would eventually come home talking with some physical limitations.

On Monday, we received a phone call from Children's Healthcare of Atlanta at Scottish Rite (CHOA) welcoming and informing us about Kendall's next phase of care. However, it was nothing like either of us thought. Kendall will be starting a "Level of Consciousness" program to help her wake up. My husband and I will simultaneously be getting trained to care for her. This pro-gram is two weeks long but may be longer; after that, we will bring Kendall home and become her caregivers 24 hours around the clock. This means both of us would be gone from our other children for two more weeks.

We were told the CHOA rehabilitation unit only provides a short stay. Once a bed becomes available, we would have less than 24 hours to get ready for the transfer. Kendall would pretty much come home in the same state that she's currently in—unconscious with a tracheostomy tube . . . a feeding tube . . . nonmobile.

Our hearts sank, and our emotions got the best of us.

Our daughter is DISabled. We were DISappointed. We were at a DISadvantage. We were DIStraught. We were DIStressed.

On Tuesday (the very next day), we met with our current social worker and her nurse. They eased our anxiety and thoroughly explained the process. In other words (as I like to say), we had a come-to-Jesus moment.

We decided to leave and get some lunch. Five minutes later, while driving, we received another call from CHOA stating that they have a bed for Kendall and the transfer will happen tomorrow (Wednesday) around 11:00 a.m. Once again, our hearts sank, and our anxiety escalated even higher than before. We had to gather seven weeks of belongings from Kennestone, tell my mama that she would be alone with three children, explain to the children what's happening, and explain the state their sister Kendall will be in when she comes home . . . the hardest daily reality. Just as we were all adjusting to our new normal, another shift of normalcy was thrown at us.

On Wednesday morning, before the tentative transfer, our children, my mama, and Rev. Bright visited Kendall because the children cannot visit her while we were at CHOA. We were saying our "see you laters" to the extraordinary team at Kennestone and preparing for our transfer. We were still anxious. Around 10:30 a.m., we received a call from CHOA saying the transfer is delayed until tomorrow.

God answered our prayers. He took our "DIS" away. Kendall is not disabled—she's ABLE. We are not disappointed—we were APPOINTED. We are not at a disadvantage—we are getting the tools to have the ADVANTAGE for Kendall's care. Not only did God take our "DIS" away, He also shifted things around. We aren't distraught—He TAUGHT us to not be anxious. We aren't distressed—this is only a TEST.

This is a MARATHON. We are still in the WARM-UP phase.

Kendall is stABLE and God is ABLE.

TWENTY-FOUR

THE BATTLE IS NOT OURS, IT'S THE LORD'S

⌘⌘⌘⌘⌘✝⌘⌘⌘⌘⌘

March 8

We've been struggling with our emotions over the past week more than ever because everything is coming to us at once— adjusting to a new hospital and all that it entails; learning to be the best caregivers for Kendall, which involves washing and dressing her, giving her medications, doing tube feeds and flushes, providing trach care, transporting her in and out of her bed and wheelchair, assisting in occupational, physical, speech, neuro, and music therapies; choosing the right program for assistance at home; having hard conversations with our attorney; parenting from afar; and realizing that bills, needs, and wants don't stop because our lives have hit a brick wall.

But in the midst of it all, we know the battle is not ours, *it's the Lord's.*

So through it all, we find peace. We find joy. We find hope. We are learning to just BREATHE . . . ONE DAY AT A TIME.

Kendall is doing well in inpatient rehabilitation. She is neuro-storming less and is responding more to less stimulation. She can see out of the right side of her right eye. She is starting to do trial runs with a tracheostomy cap. This means her tracheostomy tube is covered completely and she is breathing just like us.

It is trusting and believing in God that keeps sustaining us. It is our unquestionable and unshakable faith that gives us hope. It is the prayers and support from around the world that keep us uplifted. It is the words of inspiration, kindness, and selfless acts of strangers, friends, and family (genetics or not) that give us peace. And for all these things, we are BLESSED.

This is a MARATHON and we are still in the WARM-UP phase.

Kendall is stABLE and God is ABLE.

TWENTY-FIVE

BREATHE ON ME

⤜⤜⤜⤜⤜✝⤛⤛⤛⤛⤛

March 15

For almost seven and a half weeks, we have stared at our daughter, wondering if she can hear us, see us, feel us, or if she is hurting.

For almost seven and a half weeks, the loud noises and the beeps and the alarms coming from all of her equipment, which were so scary and annoying at times, became comforting.

For almost seven and a half weeks, we've watched and waited for her to adjust to various medication cocktails, to adjust to the weaning processes, to adjust to the sounds of her ever-changing environments and the voices of different people.

We've watched and waited for Kendall to just breathe on her own.

As we sit in this hospital, night and day, there's not a moment that goes by when we stop and wonder if today is the day we're going to BREAK.

Are we going to break because we can't pull it together, or because we are exhausted, or because we are anxious, or because the silence of the hospital room is so deafening?

The silence . . . the silence . . . the silence means no more medications through IVs, no more ventilator, no more coolant machines, no more drains for her brain, no more oxygen . . . The silence means she is progressing in a positive direction.

Kendall can BREATHE!

Every day is a new level of anxiety for us. It's similar to having a newborn baby, except Kendall's brain has to be retrained to do everything, such as swallowing, breathing, vocalizing, etc. There's a song by James Cleveland called "Breathe On Me" (please listen to it). This song has a simple message: If the breath of the Lord would just breathe on me.

No matter what you are going through—cramps, headache, body aches, cancer, death of a loved one, or something else—JUST BREATHE the breath of the Lord.

When the storms come, when the silence is deafening, when the mountains seem like they're not moving, JUST BREATHE and keep the faith.

Kendall has been making sounds over her tracheostomy tube. The miraculous part is that we shouldn't be able to hear any sounds from her until her tracheostomy tube is removed. BUT GOD knew we needed to hear her voice at seven and a half weeks.

Kendall is stABLE and God is ABLE.

TWENTY-SIX

FATHER, I STRETCH MY HANDS TO THEE

࿔࿔࿔࿔࿔✝࿔࿔࿔࿔࿔

March 18

Who knew that exactly seven years ago, the words I posted on social media then would hold true today: The human side of us always feels like what we're going through at that moment is so rough until a rougher moment comes along. That was my thought process seven years ago. But the one thing that didn't waver was my faith, because what I said back then was that God would bless us abundantly, and guess what? He did seven years later . . . spared KENDALL'S LIFE! See blessings don't necessarily come when we want them to, and they are not always financial. Blessings come in all forms, and for us, the abundance came seven years later, and the blessing was the gift of LIFE.

It was 2015, and during that time, our children were eight, seven, four, and one. My mother was living in Brunswick, Georgia. I was working over one and a half hours away from home, one way, and enduring all of our obstacles:

Team Thomas went through some trying times last month, and this month is even more trying.

My husband has to have shoulder surgery, and the healing time is six months. I need an engine in my truck. We have to move. We found all of this out within a few days of each other.

Yesterday, my husband and Kaiden (the baby) were in a head-on collision. They're okay. The van is totaled. Right now, my plate is full.

I am not going to say the devil is busy, but God is allowing things to happen as a test of our faith and the abundant blessings He has in store for us. All I keep saying is, "Father, I stretch my hands to Thee, no other help I know."

Yesterday was a hand-stretching kind of day. Late Wednesday/early Thursday morning, Kendall's oxygen level dropped into the 50s and 60s, and it should be 96 to 100%. She stopped breathing for 20-second intervals throughout that early morning. Her respiratory rate was in the 40s and it should be between 16 and 20, on average. She had to be given oxygen. I felt like I was losing my daughter before my very eyes.

My husband and I were quickly, but silently, losing it—falling apart on the inside yet trying to be strong for each other without breaking. We could see each other's frantic cry for help. We could feel each other's anxiety level rise. We were drowning.

The wrong thoughts were beginning to win in our heads, and fear was getting the best of us. Worrying. Crying. Stressing. Crying. Praying. Praying. Praying.

The doctors and the entire Comprehensive Inpatient Rehabilitation Unit (CIRU) were at a loss as well because she was doing so well. STAT labs, tests, X-rays, ultrasound, and CT scans were done. All the labs were negative/normal except Kendall's brain is swelling again.

Excess fluid had to be drained. Since her respiratory diagnostics were negative/normal, the team believes it is her brain that is causing these changes. Once the procedure was completed, Kendall had to lay flat and rest. She had a quiet rest of the day and was monitored closely. Prayerfully, this will improve her respiratory distress and set her up for a major comeback.

HER story is not done yet, and neither is God. I said it seven years ago, and I'll say it again, "Father, I stretch my hands to Thee, no other help I know." Let the BREATH of the Lord just BREATHE on Kendall, BREATHE on us, BREATHE on her doctors and her CIRU, and BREATHE on Kendall's entire prayer warriors.

Kendall is stABLE and God is ABLE.

TWENTY-SEVEN

THE STILLS

March 22

Kendall is STILL unconscious. Kendall's brain STILL has excess fluid. Kendall is STILL on oxygen. Kendall is STILL dealing with respiratory issues. Her CIRU is STILL running tests, labs, and scans, and we are STILL at a loss.

We are STILL trying not to break but hold it together. But during this season of STILLNESS, we crossed paths with three different families. One was a young mother who is going through a divorce while her autistic two-year-old daughter is hospitalized with a brain injury. PEACE BE STILL. A grandmother was thrown a curve ball when her daughter and granddaughter were in a car accident, and the granddaughter was the only survivor. Now, this grieving grandmother has to take care of her granddaughter who has a traumatic brain injury. PEACE BE STILL. A family has lost everything in a house fire and the father (a good friend of mine) is hospitalized with burns and recovering from surgery. PEACE BE STILL.

My husband and I are STILL together, closer than ever. My mother (grandmother), who is 79 years old, is STILL ABLE to help take care of our other three children while we're at the hospital. We STILL have a place to call home. Kendall is STILL alive, breathing, and is STILL progressing in other areas despite the setbacks. We simply thank God for the STILLS in our lives.

Kendall is stABLE and God is ABLE.

TWENTY-EIGHT

I Can't Imagine

෨෨෨෨෨෨✝෨෨෨෨෨෨

March 29

"I can't imagine" are the words we hear or read too often since this tragic ordeal. It's usually followed by the words, "I don't know what I would do if I were in your shoes," or "I don't know if I would be as strong as you."

Truth is, we DIDN'T IMAGINE it at all and still don't realize how strong we are. I have always mentally prepared myself for the "what ifs" of life, especially having a daughter who plays football. I anticipated the calls about broken bones or concussions.

Kendall had a concussion during the season and bounced right back. So our hearts and minds were at ease when the season ended because all was well. But 11 weeks ago, I COULDN'T EVEN IMAGINE that my life—our lives—would be changed in an instant. The "what ifs" of life I DIDN'T IMAGINE . . .

THIS. IS. US. Everyday. Seven days a week. We get up at 7:15 a.m. so that we have enough time to wash and dress ourselves and Kendall and eat breakfast before her therapy sessions, which usually start at 9:00 a.m.

She has four therapy sessions:

1. **Occupational Therapy (OT)** focuses on Kendall's ADLs (activities of daily living): washing, brushing her teeth, getting dressed, and stretching and strengthening her upper extremities and trunk. As

her caregivers, we are doing these things for her until she wakes up and can do them for herself.

2. **Physical Therapy (PT)** focuses on stretching and strengthening her lower extremities and core. As her caregivers, we are constantly stretching her.

3. **Speech Therapy** focuses on stimulating Kendall's facial muscles to help her brain relearn to use them to do things in life that come so naturally. Kendall is learning how to swallow again. A simple action that newborns aren't even taught. She also has to retrain her eyes to look to the right, left, up, and down. She has to learn how to follow and focus on an object.

4. **Music Therapy** focuses on Kendall's ability to respond to sounds.

Along with her therapy sessions, Kendall is still dealing with some setbacks in which she stops breathing for 20-second intervals, has spastic muscles, and is not consistently emptying her bladder.

Our job as husband and wife, parenting three other children from afar and assisting Grandma from afar, doesn't stop. But we hold on to our faith and each other.

We COULDN'T IMAGINE and don't want anyone else to imagine or be a part of this club.

So, we ONLY IMAGINE the awesomeness of God when the darkness comes. We ONLY IMAGINE seeing and feeling God's presence when we are anxious. We ONLY IMAGINE the beauty of God's stillness when the quietness seems the loudest. We ONLY IMAGINE the greatness of God when we need peace, comfort, and understanding. We ONLY IMAGINE the day Kendall will wake up and be made whole again.

WE CAN ONLY IMAGINE.

Kendall is stABLE and God is ABLE.

SECOND QUARTER

TWENTY-NINE

IF I COULD TURN
BACK THE HANDS OF TIME

ôôôôôô✝ôôôôô

April 5

One of the hardest parts of this journey is the social media memories (traditions in general). It takes me—it takes us—back into times of happiness, joy, and laughter. It takes me back to some of our favorite moments in life—cruising, celebrating, and just being us—Team Thomas . . . a party of seven . . . always together. These precious memories display all of us talking, walking, eating, laughing, and dancing. Together. And even those social media memories that take us back to the hard times of life—sickness, minor accidents, surgeries, and even death of loved ones, you will still find us—Team Thomas . . . a party of seven . . . always together.

As I reflect on the past 12 weeks, I often think, *If I could turn back the hands of time* . . . Kendall would be following me foot to foot. She would be in my face. She would be talking my head off. She would be laughing, eating, and burping loudly. She would be the life of the party—the social butterfly. She would be #43 on that football field. She would be that dancer at church, slightly off cue because she's looking for me. IF I COULD TURN BACK THE HANDS OF TIME . . . Kendall. Kendall. Kendall.

I can almost see, taste, hear, feel, and smell those memories be-cause they're so overwhelming, now more than ever. IF I COULD TURN BACK THE HANDS OF TIME. But that is the selfish side of me; it's human nature to want what we had, to long for what we lost, to yearn for more time.

But IF I COULD TURN BACK THE HANDS OF TIME, I wouldn't know how strong my faith is. I wouldn't know how prayers and love truly have no color. I wouldn't know the depths of the kindness of strangers. I wouldn't know the effects and the affects of the full power of Prayer. I wouldn't know what the BREATHS and the STILLS of life meant.

IF I COULD TURN BACK THE HANDS OF TIME, I wouldn't know that Kendall's story turned so many people to God. I wouldn't know that nonbelievers prayed. I wouldn't know that this journey is not just for us. I wouldn't know how it feels to be carried by God. I wouldn't know . . .

Kendall is progressing well, but she still struggles with some respiratory issues at night. She is still unconscious, but she is becoming more awake. It is difficult to determine what her brain activity is until she speaks.

Kendall's temporal lobe was the area that was damaged during this tragic accident. That part of the brain is primarily responsible for language and memory—long and short. We're not sure if she knows us, but right now we are familiar to her because she sees and hears us the most.

Kendall is stABLE and God is ABLE.

THIRTY

THROUGH IT ALL

⤿⤿⤿⤿⤿✝⤾⤾⤾⤾⤾

April 12

My world was turned upside down 13 weeks ago. My daughter, Kendall, was no longer that bubbly burst of energy and that ray of sunshine. She was no longer that sweet spirit that lit up a room. She was no longer that talkative, compassionate soul. She was no longer that girl who played football. Kendall was no longer . . .

She was my daughter who was struck by a vehicle at school, flying up in the air, landing on her head, and losing consciousness in front of her 11-year-old brother . . . an image I can't shake, a feeling I hate feeling, a pain I can't medicate.

She went from talking, walking, running, eating, and laughing to a body of dead weight functioning and surviving off of machines. She was no longer . . . and all I could do was cry out, "JESUS. JESUS. JESUS."

I know the power of worldwide prayers. I've been praying for a light in the darkness. I know there's a calm before the storm. I know unconditional love and what happens when praises go up.

But what happens when I, the strong one, experience the unexpected and try to fight a battle that belongs to the Lord? I've asked God to just breathe on me. I've thanked Him for the stills. But all I do is imagine myself turning back the hands of time. Every day I look in the mirror or stand motionless in the shower and I tell myself, *I've cried my last tears yesterday*. Then my yesterday becomes today, and my today becomes tomorrow, and I find myself drowning. Through my smile, I'm crying. Through my laughter, I'm screaming. Through my joy, I'm hurting. Through my "Okays," I'm struggling.

I find myself trying to function just enough to get through "the firsts." The first birthday celebration, the first spring break, the first Sunday, the first holiday . . . without the Kendall we know. I'm grieving a loss that I didn't lose. I'm grieving what was because of what it is now. I feel helpless. The more I grieve, the more I hurt. The more I cry, the closer I am to God, and that is a beauty all in itself.

Through it all, I'm still encouraged. Through it all, I'm still thankful for God using me, using my family—Team Thomas. Through it all, I'm learning to lean and depend on God. Through it all, I will shout, "Hallelujah Anyhow!" Thanks, Rev. Bright!

Due to Kendall's respiratory issues, she had a sleep study performed Sunday night, and it was determined that she had some type of obstruction in her airways. She will have a bronchoscopy to view her airways. If the obstruction can be removed surgically, they will do so. If her airways are clear, then she will need to sleep with a BiPAP machine, which is similar to a CPAP machine for sleep apnea.

Kendall is still fighting and is getting stronger every day despite her nightly respiratory issues. She is able to respond to stimulation, with some responses being purposeful and some being reflexive.

Kendall initially was getting discharged on Wednesday, which is still a possibility depending on the bronchoscopy. While this should (and is) a joyous occasion, it is also overwhelming (trying to keep Kendall on a schedule and blending in the rest of Team Thomas). Although we are anxious, we have done everything we can to be an advocate for Kendall and to be the best caregivers for her.

Kendall is stABLE and God is ABLE.

THIRTY-ONE

KENDALL'S DISCHARGE DAY

ॐॐॐॐॐ✝ॐॐॐॐॐ

April 19

Today is the day that we have longed for; it is the day that we have waited for; it is the day we all have prayed for . . . Discharge Day! And while thousands around this world are shouting, "Hallelujah!" and screaming, "Thank you, JESUS!" and crying tears of joy, my husband and I are in a state of uneasiness and apprehension. So many questions and doubts started flooding our minds. Paranoia is at an all-time high. Our anxiety levels have once again risen. And we find ourselves feeling ill at ease and lost.

You see, when Kendall was initially hospitalized, we were devastated and depressed. We were yearning and longing for answers. All we wanted and needed was for our baby girl to JUST. WAKE. UP. But she couldn't, and our baby girl became a daily image of drains, IVs, catheters, wires, bandages, tubes—this was our new normal.

The stillness of Kendall and the unsynchronized beeps of the alarms began to pacify our heartache. Just as we got comfortable and accepted our new normal, God shifted things. Kendall was ready for rehabilitation. Once again, we found ourselves on an emotional roller coaster, and we were headed mentally in a downward spiral. More questions. New concerns. The fear of the unknown had gotten the best of us. We couldn't see that Kendall was progressing. We couldn't get outside of our heads.

After seven weeks of inpatient rehabilitation and seven weeks of training, we had adjusted to our new environment and made it our "home." And like clockwork, after each and every tentative discharge date (five to be exact), we went through this internal turmoil over and over again.

Just when we were ready to let go, God's Mercy and His Grace kept us. Our new level of anxiety became our new level of hope. Our pain became joy. Our restlessness became peace. Our doubts became faith. Our new normal became our test, and our test is becoming our testimony.

Kendall is stABLE and God is ABLE.

THIRTY-TWO

There's a Sweet Spirit in This Place

✿✿✿✿✿ † ✿✿✿✿✿

April 26

Kendall has been home for exactly one week, and although we are truly overjoyed, we are also extremely exhausted.

My husband and I have stepped into full caregiver mode, and my mama-bear instincts are at an all-time high.

For 14 weeks, various doctors, nurses, techs, and therapists have cared for Kendall, and we had options (for the last seven weeks) to assist or not. We had the option to give medications or not. We had the option to start her feed or not. We had the option to change her diapers or not. We had the option to give her a shower or not. We had the option to assist with speech, occupational, physical, and music therapies or not. We had options.

What I am learning through this chapter of my life is that we take options for granted and when those options are taken away, will we have a spirit of fear, or will we have a spirit of *no weapon formed against us shall prosper*?

I kept telling myself for weeks that I'm so ready to leave this hospital. I'm so ready to take my baby home. I'm so ready to see my other babies and my mama. I'm so ready for Team Thomas, party of seven, to be under one roof again. But was I really ready?

Every morning in the shower, I would just stand motionless and cry uncontrollably, wondering if I have enough strength to weather this storm. Am I equipped to give Kendall what she needs? Will I be able to balance being a full-time caregiver and still be a mother, a wife, and a daughter? Am I enough?

When we stepped into our house with Kendall and saw pure innocence and peace on her face, we knew we were ready for this enormous task ahead of us. We watched her smile so easily when she saw her siblings (especially Camryn) and her grandmother. At that moment, a sweet, sweet spirit filled this place, and I knew that God was present.

For the first time in 14 weeks, I was in a place of serenity. I had fallen in love with God all over again, and it felt so good. At that moment, no matter how anxious, depressed, or devastated we had been, I knew God had never left us. He never failed us. He has and will always be our way maker, our miracle worker, our promise keeper, our light in the darkness.

Kendall is stABLE and God is ABLE.

THIRTY-THREE

Prayers of Yesterday, Today, and Tomorrow

᭗᭗᭗᭗᭗✝᭗᭗᭗᭗᭗

May 3

The past 16 weeks of my life can be best summarized by the first line in Charles Dickens's book, *A Tale of Two Cities*: "It was the best of times, it was the worst of times."

The night before her horrific accident, Kendall was just eating, talking, laughing, and watching the Georgia vs. Alabama game. We were talking trash to each other because half of us were rooting for Alabama. And, although I was in quarantine because of COVID, she made me feel like I was right there watching the game with the rest of Team Thomas. We were having the time of our lives. She was having the time of her life.

But this particular night, Kendall was tired and went to bed early without finishing watching the game. She came to my room door, and we exchanged our usual "good night" and "I love you."

The very next day, my husband received a call that shattered our souls into a million pieces. Who knew that after that night, it would be a while before I would ever hear her voice again and feel her radiant personality. It was the best of times; it was the worst of times.

January 11, 2022, could have broken us beyond repair. It could have destroyed our marriage. It could have caused us to lose our faith in God. It could have had us questioning God. It could have been Kendall's sunset date.

There are things that happen to us in which God is trying to teach us something—perhaps to learn from our mistakes. And there are things that happen to us, but that are not for us. Sometimes, God chooses us to go through some things for others to see His glory.

I know that on January 11, 2022, God chose Team Thomas. This road has not been easy. We have bad days. We have weak moments. We have times when we want to throw in the towel, but we can't. WE. ARE. EXHAUSTED.

But one thing I know—we are surviving off of the prayers of YESTERDAY . . . the prayers our mothers, grandparents, and great-grandparents prayed for us. These are the prayers and blessings that God promised them. We are surviving off of the prayers of TODAY . . . prayers that are being said around the world for Kendall and us daily. These are the prayers that are carrying us in our time of anxiousness, weakness, and depression. We are surviving off of the prayers of TOMORROW . . . prayers that thank God in advance for what He is going to do and what we know in our hearts is already done. These are the prayers we pray for our children's children.

This season has been nothing but blessings after blessings. We refuse to let our circumstance steal our joy and stop us from praising God. It is our best season during our worst season. Just when I hit my lowest point, God gives me a taste of what He is capable of.

Kendall is stABLE and God is ABLE.

THIRTY-FOUR

A MOTHER'S DAY

May 10

We, like many families, celebrate most holidays. It's a time of joy and thankfulness; it's a time when families come together, eat, drink, and be merry. I can almost hear the laughter of kids, smell the aroma from the kitchen, and feel the love in the atmosphere.

No matter the holiday, the vibe at our house was always the same—family, food, and fun. But this year, the holidays aren't quite the same. There's one less plate at the table, one less loud voice, one less child running around, one less homemade Mother's Day gift . . . ONE LESS. ONE LESS. ONE LESS.

I always looked forward to the month of May because it's my birth month and Mother's Day. It's the ONE day of the year I don't MOTHER. I usually hibernate in my room, get waited on hand and foot, get served drinks and appetizers, and make a guest appearance once my elaborate dinner is done. My husband and children would spend hours making the perfect meal and pampering and treating me like royalty. All four of my children would try to outdo each other to see who would be my favorite child that day while my husband gives me the world.

But *this* Mother's Day was different. I struggled. Nothing went according to plan. Nothing about this holiday was traditional. Nothing felt right. I really didn't want to do anything. But I put on my happy face, got dressed, and went to church while my husband stayed home with Kendall.

The whole time in church, I'm smiling, singing, and praising God physically—but mentally, I just wanted to run out, cry, and scream, because *this* was too much. My youngest daughter, Kaiden (age eight), was trying to console me, and my mother was on standby.

All I wanted and needed was the ONE MORE I was missing. Then I heard the testimony of our minister of music. When he could do nothing else, he just whispered, "Jesus, Jesus, Jesus." At that moment, every emotion that I had been feeling and suppressing for weeks came to the surface. I couldn't stop the tears until my soul was cleansed. I couldn't stop the tears until my faith was refreshed. I couldn't stop the tears until I whispered, "Jesus, Jesus, Jesus."

I looked at my mother in admiration, and I knew everything was going to be all right because the message was simple:

> *Because of her . . . I am . . .*
> *Because of her unconditional love, I am nurturing.*
> *Because of her faith, I am able to persevere.*
> *Because of her willingness, I am strong.*
> *Because of her determination, I am unstoppable.*

Now replace the word "her" with "God." Whether you are the "because of her" or the "I am," nothing is impossible for our God. There are many who are hurting, but remember, because of His love, you are . . . I am . . .

Kendall is stABLE and God is ABLE.

THIRTY-FIVE

Rise Up!

⤖⤖⤖⤖⤖✝⤖⤖⤖⤖⤖

May 17

This whole journey so far has been nothing but triumphs out of a tragedy. It has not only changed our lives forever but it has changed lives across the world. It has taught me not to question God and to continue to share our testimony.

Yes, I still hurt. I still cry uncontrollably daily. I still have moments of weakness and lessened faith where I want to turn back the hands of time. I still think about the "shouldas," the "couldas," the "wouldas," and the "what ifs." But the most important still is that I STILL have Kendall on this side.

I am learning to find peace in the midst of my storms, love in the midst of my heartaches, joy in the midst of my pain, understanding in the midst of my confusion, and hope in the midst of my disappointments.

God chose us for a reason, and if God should happen to be done telling His story through us today, then my soul will be at peace knowing Kendall's journey has brought so many people closer to Him and increased their faith.

But God is not through with us yet. He chose us—Team Thomas. Why? The answer is simple . . . to RISE UP.

RISE UP and share our love for God.

RISE UP and show our unwavering faith.

RISE UP and show the incredible strength that we didn't know we had.

RISE UP and praise God for the good, the bad, and the ugly.

RISE UP to the unexpected.

RISE UP and shout, "Hallelujah Anyhow!"

RISE UP and continue to thank God despite our circumstances.

RISE UP so that Kendall one day will RISE UP.

So that Kendall one day will RISE UP.

So that Kendall one day will RISE UP.

From last Friday until today, so many people ROSE UP for Kendall. She fist-bumped all of her football teammates, went to church (Turner Chapel AME Church), and had a one-on-one visit with Freddie the Falcon from the Atlanta Falcons. We are so grateful for the blessings beyond measure we have received from the beginning of this journey from everyone.

RISE UP!

Kendall is stABLE and God is ABLE.

THIRTY-SIX

GOD'S TIMING

ᕗᕗᕗᕗᕗ✝ᕘᕘᕘᕘᕘ

May 24

For over a month, my neighborhood had been planning a rally for Kendall in Acworth, Georgia. It was going to be a family-filled event with various vendors and talks about safe teen driving and awareness. It was set for May 21, 2022.

Around the same time (unbeknownst to me) on the other side of town (Decatur, Georgia), the Atlanta Phoenix Women's Football Team had been planning something special for Kendall during their halftime show at their last home game. It was also scheduled for May 21. It was going to be a big day for Team Thomas and an even bigger day for Kendall. Somehow, someway, we were going to make appearances at both events with Kendall to show our heartfelt gratitude to a community that had carried us thus far. It was going to be epic! (*Man plans . . .*)

The closer it was to May 21, the more anxious we were. It was a good, but nervous, energy. We were ready and had been telling Kendall all about her big day coming up. We planned for every possible scenario but this one . . .

On Friday, May 13, Kendall began vomiting daily shortly after her feeds. By Sunday, May 15, Kendall's stomach was hard and swollen. We did everything we knew how to do, including adjusting her feeds and water intake and making sure her bowels were moving. But it wasn't enough. By Wednesday morning, May 18, we felt defeated and took Kendall to urgent care. They immediately sent us to the ER where Kendall was admitted. We were in disbelief. We thought the doctors would just X-ray Kendall's abdomen, give us a bowel regimen, and send us on our merry little way. (*Man plans . . .*)

We had big plans on May 21. Kendall couldn't miss two retired, professional football players, Freddie the Falcon, a local rapper, the Atlanta Phoenix Women's Football Game, and a host of others. It was Kendall Day, and the world was anticipating her arrival. And WE WERE READY. (*Man plans . . .*)

Kendall was in the hospital from Wednesday until Sunday. Needless to say, she did not make Kendall Day. However, all festivities proceeded, and Team Thomas, party of six (not seven), made it to both events to represent Kendall.

Kendall's hospital stay was a blessing in disguise. It was the first time since Kendall was discharged from the hospital (April 19) that we finally slept longer than four hours. We still don't have nursing assistance because there's a shortage of home healthcare nurses, and one nurse was not the right fit.

My husband and I are her sole caregivers. Our day starts at 5:50 a.m. and ends around 1:30-2:00 a.m. This is daily. NO DAYS OFF.

I believe, during this whole experience, God is coaching Kendall and she is running HIS plays. When we learned we had two weeks to learn how to care for Kendall (in inpatient rehabilitation), we were overwhelmed, angry, and anxious. God said, "Kendall, start waking up slowly so that your stay will be longer and your parents will be at ease." GOD'S TIMING.

When we needed the right respiratory equipment for Kendall but every avenue the doctors tried failed, God said, "Kendall, I need you to struggle breathing at night so bad that it gives the doctors the right data they need for their report, and you will get discharged with the proper respiratory equipment." GOD'S TIMING.

When we were tired, weary, and exhausted, God said, "Kendall, I need you to have some digestive issues major enough to get hospitalized but minor enough to have NOTHING wrong so that your resilient and strong parents can rest." GOD'S TIMING.

I could go on and on.

We may make plans that are so perfectly thought out, but our plans mean nothing when God is in control. God knows what's best and moves on *His* time. Well, today, we are especially relying on GOD'S TIMING. Kendall is having surgery this morning at 11:00 a.m. to put her skull back on the right side of her brain. Please continue to lift her up in prayer.

Kendall is stABLE and God is ABLE.

THIRTY-SEVEN

KENDALL'S THIRD BRAIN SURGERY

৵৵৵৵৵✝৵৵৵৵৵

May 25

Yesterday, Kendall had cranioplasty surgery to put her skull back on the right side of her brain. Her surgery was a success! She has to overcome some obstacles, but she's headed in the right direction. She has two drains in her head—one to drain the excess blood, and the other to drain excess fluid due to her brain swelling.

She was severely dehydrated, so her feeds will be adjusted to a tolerable level. She is alert, but her heart rate is elevated. A few factors contribute to her increase in heart rate, such as pain, awareness, and shifting of fluid in her brain. She will experience several painful headaches, which is common after this procedure. Since she is becoming more awake, she will get easily agitated.

She is unaware of what has happened to her, and her surroundings are different now. She has to adjust to her "new" skull on the right side, which has been off since January 11, 2022. The shift of fluid will affect her responses to any and all stimuli.

Her eyes move swiftly back and forth occasionally, and then she will stop and fixate on us. We can tell she's trying to figure out what is going on.

As a parent, it's hard to watch. How do I comfort my daughter when I don't know what's troubling her at the moment? But I know the same God that comforts, heals, and brings peace to me will do the same for Kendall.

Thank you for your continuous prayers and support.

Kendall is stABLE and God is ABLE.

THIRTY-EIGHT

THERE'S SOMETHING ABOUT TUESDAYS

❦❦❦❦❦✝❦❦❦❦❦

May 31

Tuesdays are rough for me. It's the one day of the week that I dread. It's the one day of the week I hate. It's a constant reminder of Kendall's unimaginable accident. It marks the one day of the week that I couldn't be there for Kendall when she needed my protection the most. It marks the one day of the week that I couldn't be there for my son, Chase, when he needed me to shield him the most. It marks the one day of the week that I couldn't comfort my other children when they needed me the most. It marks the one day of the week that I couldn't be with my husband when we needed each other's love the most. It marks the one day of the week that I couldn't be with my mother when I needed her arms around me the most.

I hate Tuesdays. Every Tuesday, time stands still and a sickening feeling overshadows my soul that I can't shake.

I hate Tuesdays. It's the day my daughter Kendall went from a vibrant soul to an unconscious, motionless being. It's the day she was fighting for her life and overcoming two emergency brain surgeries without me . . . her mama.

I hate Tuesdays. Days leading up to Tuesdays, I would feel myself getting restless trying to figure out a way to bypass them.

I hate Tuesdays. It's the loudest day of the week. *Lord, my God, why Tuesday?*

But God heard my cries and felt my pain. He knew I needed to remove this hate from my heart. So, He turned my Tuesdays into days of serenity.

He gave me this incredible strength to share my innermost thoughts with the world on Tuesdays. People all over the world bombard Heaven with prayers for Kendall, myself, my husband, and the rest of my family on Tuesdays. Kendall had two successful brain surgeries on a Tuesday. She was discharged from the in-patient rehabilitation facility on a Tuesday. Kendall's first sign of following commands was on a Tuesday. She had a third successful brain surgery on a Tuesday. And a new chapter in my life — Chapter 44, is today, a Tuesday. Happy birthday to me!

Although Tuesdays are still tough for me, I know that God has great plans for Team Thomas. These Tuesday prayers mean more to me than you'll ever imagine because I hated Tuesdays.

Kendall has been in the hospital since last Tuesday. During that time, I was also hospitalized for a short stay. All of a sudden, I felt hot with a squeezing and heaviness of my chest. That was followed by chest pains that radiated to my left shoulder. I couldn't focus. Thank God I was already at the hospital and was immediately tended to. All is well. Just when I thought I was managing my stress as well as one can under these circumstances, my body said something different.

As for Kendall, her skull was successfully placed back on the right side of her brain. She is still being monitored due to swelling in her brain and feeding issues. She is recovering well.

Kendall is stABLE and God is ABLE.

THIRTY-NINE

PLEASE DON'T TAKE MY SUNSHINE AWAY

❧❧❧❧❧✝❧❧❧❧❧

June 7

For almost two weeks, I have been reevaluating myself since I was hospitalized for stress. I'm trying to figure out how to better cope with our new normal. I mean, I thought I had it all together. I prayed. I screamed. I shouted. I cried. I wouldn't eat. I couldn't sleep. I was there for my husband. I was there for my children. I was there for Kendall. I leaned on my mother. I was present for others. I put all of us in therapy. I held on to my faith. I wrote it out. I talked it out. I was silent. I leaned on God. I called on Jesus. I was touched by the Holy Spirit. And yet, those things were not enough . . . because I still found myself held in bondage by stress.

I wasn't coping with our new normal. I was just putting on a face and going with the flow because I didn't want a pity party. Pity parties lead to accepting what is *stalling* and not anticipating what will be *progressing*. Pity parties will slowly pick you apart and lead you down a road of self-sabotage. Pity parties will have you questioning God and losing your faith in Him. I didn't want a pity party. I'm all cried out. I'm exhausted. I feel helpless. My God, what am I not doing?

I had an overdue conversation with a dear sistafriend of mine yesterday. She brought up the biblical parable of the woman with the issue of blood who bled for 12 years. My sistafriend asked,

"What if that woman's issue of blood wasn't literally blood, but what if it was blood meaning family? What if she had been dealing with family drama for 12 years and just needed help breaking generational curses? What if her issue of blood was her bad choices in life? What if her issue of blood was trying to be perfect in an imperfect world?" She said, "Shanna, you have been doing everything but dealing with your own issue of blood. What has God been calling you to do these past 21 weeks?" This hit me hard.

As she was continuing to speak, tears just flowed down my face, and I knew at that moment my issue of blood was not just Kendall's accident. My issue of blood was deeper than that. God has put an unexpected calling on my life as many of you have mentioned several times. And until I listen and do His work, I will always have this issue of blood.

Kendall's accident was no mistake. It was a horrific and heart-breaking tragedy, but it has been a powerful act of God that has led so many back to Him and renewed faith in others. God has given me incredible strength that I have been able to display through writing, and it is nothing but the blood.

I have been in constant battle with myself trying to keep it together. I still cry uncontrollably. I still feel defeated at times. I still feel anxious. I still struggle. But then I look at Kendall, and I sing this song by Jimmie Davis:

> *You are my sunshine, my only sunshine.*
> *You make me happy when skies are gray.*
> *You'll never know dear how much I love you.*
> *Please don't take my sunshine away.*

For the past two weeks, I've prayed that my SONshine will not be taken away. Whatever your issue of blood is, don't let it take your SONshine away.

Kendall is still in the hospital. Continue to pray that the blood in her head gets reabsorbed by her brain. Pray that this third formula agrees with her digestive system. Pray that her heart rate and blood pressure stabilize. Pray that the left side of her body wakes up and starts to move purposefully. Pray that she stops grinding her teeth and that she will open her mouth and learn to swallow. Pray that she speaks. Pray that she walks. Pray that she wakes up completely in her right mind. Pray that her nightmares go away. Pray for Kendall. Pray for our SUNSHINE. For I am grateful that our SONshine did not take our SUNSHINE away.

Kendall is stABLE and God is ABLE.

FORTY

It's Bittersweet

❧❧❧❧❧✝❧❧❧❧❧

June 14

I've been on this emotional roller coaster for 22 weeks, but this past week has just been a merry-go-round of anxiety, anger, disappointment, and frustration. I don't know if I'm coming or going, and I don't have the energy to get off this ride. I feel hopeless and defeated.

You see, when Kendall was initially hospitalized on January 11, 2022, we were told that she would go to the Shepherd Center for inpatient rehabilitation. Unfortunately, she was denied because she needed to be alert for three hours and a Level III on the Rancho Los Amigos Levels of Cognitive Functioning Scale.

At that time, Kendall was completely unconscious and not alert. Therefore, she was sent to CHOA. During her seven weeks of rehabilitation, Kendall progressed well and left there alert and aware. My husband and I were ecstatic. We were overjoyed because we knew firsthand where Kendall started.

We watched her day by day, hour by hour, and minute by minute go from unconscious with no response to stimuli, to minimally conscious with response to stimuli. We were riding on this high and were feeling unstoppable. Although we were functioning on four to five hours of sleep, my husband and I had mastered our caregiving routine, and Kendall was thriving more once we were home.

A month later, we found ourselves with Kendall back in the

hospital—four weeks so far. The first week was unexpected due to her vomiting issues, and what was supposed to be a three-day stay following her brain surgery turned into a three-week stay.

Despite this setback, we were still hopeful. We saw this as an opportunity to finally get Kendall into the Shepherd Center. There's no way she could be denied. She is alert and aware. She is up for well over three hours and is a Level III.

Well . . . well . . . well . . . the Shepherd Center denied Kendall again because now she needs to be at a Level IV and CHOA said she needed to be at a Level V to return. This is when WE LOST IT!

For the first time during this whole unimaginable accident, I began to question God. I have the faith. I'm putting in the work. I'm giving beyond my all. Yet I keep hitting brick walls. What frustrates me the most is that the politics of these rehabilitation facilities were unfolding right before my eyes. Why can't they see Kendall through my eyes and feel the compassion and determination in my heart? How can they be so cutthroat and ruthless? They are considered one of the best rehabilitation facilities, yet the very same traumatic brain injury patients they love to help are the same ones they have no problem turning their backs on.

Where do the Kendalls of the world go? Who do they turn to? How do we as parents and caregivers stay strong and keep fighting? Why won't these rehabilitation facilities like the Shephard Center take her? Do we need to look outside of Georgia? LORD, HEAR MY CRY! What shall I do?

Today is a bittersweet Tuesday. Today, Team Thomas, party of seven, was supposed to be departing for Hawaii for 10 days of paradise. It was going to be the first time the kids flew (two flew as babies). It was going to be a trip in which we were going to celebrate three milestones—Camryn's Sweet 16, our 15th wedding anniversary, and my mother's 80th birthday. This was our year!

We were longing for our annual big trip as we have been cruising every year for Christmas since 2017.

When the pandemic hit in 2020, we agreed to take a big trip in 2022 because, of course, by then the pandemic would be over. By

November 2021, we had paid for the plane tickets and half of the resort balance. We were ready for Hawaii! Then January 11, 2022, happened, and Team Thomas's (party of seven) world was turned upside down, and our hearts were shattered into pieces.

Someday we'll get to Hawaii as a party of seven, enjoying a taste of paradise. But God has bigger plans for us, and I know the blessings, my testimony, and Kendall's outcome are going to be the sweetest taste of paradise.

I am worn out and exhausted, but God will replenish my soul and renew my strength. We will find the best rehabilitation facility for Kendall, but in the meantime, we will keep pushing through these mountains and wait on the Lord.

This is a MARATHON, and I have to let go and let God. When I get down and out, I look at Kendall and ask, "Kendall strong?" And with a smile, Kendall shows me her strength by flexing her right bicep. If Kendall is strong, then I am strong.

Kendall is stABLE and God is ABLE.

FORTY-ONE

A FATHER'S LOVE

৵৵৵৵৵✝৵৵৵৵৵

June 21

Two days ago, the entire nation celebrated Father's Day. It was a day we honored and/or cherished precious memories of our biological fathers, stepfathers, father figures, perfect fathers, imperfect fathers, and just men in general.

It is one of many occasions that I put my husband on a pedestal for the world to just get a glimpse of what I have the pleasure of experiencing daily. His love for our children is unconditional and limitless. He gives of himself effortlessly and will move heaven and earth for our children. His world revolves around our children, and they are the rhythm of his heart. But this Father's Day was different because we're still struggling with our new normal.

I tried to keep up appearances and embrace some sense of normalcy. We went to church, and I cooked my husband's traditional Father's Day dinner: oxtails, fried ribs, BBQ ribs, rice, black-eyed peas, cabbage, mac 'n' cheese, candied yams, potato salad, cornbread, and our oldest daughter made desserts—apple turnovers and brownies. We had family over for dinner, and my husband opened his gifts. The sounds of great music, laughter, and love filled the house as we ate and drank. But no matter how much we looked the part, we were hurting on the inside.

Behind my husband's eyes, I could see his pain. I could feel his heartache. I could taste his tears. I could hear his cry. I could smell his anger.

A father's job is to protect and provide for his family, and when those things are taken from a man, especially due to circumstances beyond his control, it will destroy a man and weaken his soul.

I watch my husband, day in and day out, push Kendall to get stronger and encourage her to keep fighting, but I can tell the revolving door of progress, setbacks, and comebacks were starting to get the best of him. My fear was that my husband would break any day now and this would be the one time I can't mend his agony. But when a man has the love of God our Father inside of him, then nothing formed against him shall prosper.

The same love that my husband has for our children is the same love that God has for us. God's Love, Grace, and Mercy brought us through this moment, and He will continue to carry us through.

Unfortunately, Kendall's brain is not able to reabsorb any cerebral spinal fluid (CSF) or brain fluid. The swelling of her brain is increasing. This morning, Kendall will undergo her fourth brain surgery to have a shunt put in her skull to drain the excess fluid. The catheter from the shunt will go from her brain to her abdomen. This shunt is *permanent*. If she does not have this surgery, she will decline neurologically and would not be eligible for inpatient rehabilitation.

Please pray for her neurosurgeon, his assistant, who is the general surgeon, and the entire surgical team. Pray for Kendall's protection, healing, and recovery. Pray for the renewing of our strength and removing our anxiety as parents. Pray for my mother, Evelyn, and our children, Camryn, Chase, and Kaiden. Pray for admission to the Shepherd Center for Kendall for inpatient rehabilitation. Pray for yourselves and pray for each other. Thank God for the revolving doors of life and the emotional roller coasters.

Kendall is stABLE and God is ABLE.

FORTY-TWO

AHHH

᚛᚛᚛᚛᚛ † ᚛᚛᚛᚛᚛

June 28

The Shepherd Center is ranked in the top 10 of rehabilitation hospitals in the nation, specializing in brain and spinal cord injuries. According to the center's website, patients get more than just medical care—they get an experience that brings healing and hope.

The Shepherd Center is dedicated to helping its patients rebuild their lives with hope, independence, and dignity, advocating for their full inclusion in all aspects of community life. Their comprehensive brain injury rehabilitation program treats specific conditions, such as disorders of consciousness, and specific age groups, such as teenagers. To simplify, Kendall is their ideal patient. Yet she has been denied not once, not twice, not three times. On the fourth denial, the administration just said to try CHOA since she did so well there. At that time, CHOA required Kendall to be at a Level V, which was a higher level than what Shepherd required.

For weeks, we have been fighting, advocating, crying, pleading, and yearning for help. Doors kept getting slammed in our faces. Even Kendall's extraordinary neurosurgeon was going above and beyond trying to get Kendall into Shepherd. And he was getting knocked down, and he was getting frustrated. I was even looking at facilities outside of Georgia. I was ready to plead with anyone who knew Oprah, Tyler Perry, Will Packer, Angela White, Lisa Diane Washington, or any celebrity who could get

Kendall the help she needs, because the denials had more to do with money and insurance than the desire and capability to help. The politics of these facilities . . . our hearts kept getting stomped on, and our glimmer of hope kept getting dimmer.

I didn't know if we were being impatient and not waiting on God, or if we were fighting so hard for Kendall and refusing to just settle, because there's a fine line between the two. I kept thinking, *What good is faith if we don't put the work in?* But at that point, I was starting to break. Was I just using the scripture to justify my aggressive actions? Was I doing more harm than good? How much fight do I have left? I know I am mentally and physically breaking.

I'm longing for a change of scenery. I'm longing for a family vacation. I'm longing for time with my husband. I'm longing for my mother to have a much-needed vacation with her friends. I'm longing for the ability to work one to two days a week. I'm longing for a breakthrough, no matter how big or small. I'm longing for happiness, peace, and joy. I'm longing for stability. I'm longing for answers. I'm longing for my four children to be together again. I'm longing for my heart to be healed.

On January 11, 2022, the best of Kendall was taken away. The neurosurgeon and his entire neuro team gave their best to surgically repair Kendall. Kendall received the best inpatient care at CHOA. My husband and I give Kendall our best daily. So why wouldn't we want to continue this road to recovery with the proclaimed best rehabilitation center, Shepherd Center?

I had to take a step back because I knew I was getting closer to that dark place that I may not recover from. So, we took the weekend off from consuming our minds with the "what ifs," the "why nots," and "how comes." We simply asked God for a sign that everything was going to be all right.

Early Sunday morning around 12:30 a.m., Kendall said, "Ahhh." Although she was getting ice chips rubbed on her lips at the time, she has never been vocal about it. The word "ah" means a realization—*there you are*. There You are . . . God was there.

When the Real Doctor, God, lives in the fleshly doctor, the neuro-surgeon, who matches the same fighting spirit as God-fearing parents of a child who is blessed and has a multitude of prayer warriors, God will make the first last and the last first.

Yesterday, the neurosurgeon told us CHOA had accepted Kendall back into its inpatient rehabilitation program; CHOA, which was the last and required a higher level of consciousness than the first, Shepherd.

Thank God for the last. Thank God for the many denials. Thank God for shifting the atmosphere. Thank you, God, for the "Ahhh."

Kendall is stABLE and God is ABLE.

HALFTIME

FORTY-THREE

IN THE STILL OF THE NIGHT

✺✺✺✺✺✺†✺✺✺✺✺✺

July 5

For 25 weeks, my darkest moments are in the still of the night. It is when the human side of me battles the spiritual side of me and collision is so earth-shattering at times. The human side of me struggles to find peace because the stillness of the night seems so chaotic. My mind wanders down a path of wrong thoughts and anger finds her way in once again. In the stillness of the night, as I gaze at Kendall, pondering what once was, I began to slowly crumble because I'm yearning to hear her speak. I'm yearning to hear her laugh. I'm yearning to see her eat. I'm yearning to see her walk. I'm yearning for her to hug me. I'm yearning for Kendall to come back to me.

My pain is daily. It is a continuous hurt in which the frequency is constant but the intensity varies. You see, I muster up enough strength to dress up my outer appearance. I do it so well that if you didn't know me, you wouldn't know what I've been going through. But on the inside, my head is spinning. I'm blinded by tears. I'm nauseous. I'm trying to mend a broken heart. My stomach is in knots. My limbs go limp. And my spirit gets derailed. Then in the still of the night, my "strong" outer appearance gets overshadowed by my inner appearance, and I begin to mentally drown.

Just when I'm on the brink of breaking, God whispers in my ear, "You are blessed. Count your blessings." So, I started listing my blessings: I woke up this morning. I have food, clothes, and shelter. My husband and I haven't worked since Kendall's accident, but the bills are paid. I have transportation. My mother and children are safe. I kept listing, but God said dig deeper and COUNT your blessings.

I looked at Kendall, and I said, "God, I thank you for keeping Kendall on this side of the earth. God, I thank you for giving Kendall the ability to look up, down, to the left, and to the right. God, I thank you for Kendall's ability to follow simple commands. God, I thank you for her ability to swallow tiny drops of water. God, I thank you for Kendall's ability to move the entire right side of her body. God, I thank you for giving us a way to communicate with our daughter. God, I thank you for Kendall's entire neuro and critical care teams. God, I thank you for allowing Kendall to be more conscious. God, I thank you, because on January 11, 2022, the only blessing I could count was, "Thank you for allowing us to *see* Kendall and not *view* her." Now my "in the still of the nights" are my "in the midnight hours."

Kendall has been safely transported to CHOA. We are getting settled in. It's bittersweet because we're in the same room from the first round of inpatient rehabilitation. Thank you for your continuous prayers and support. May God bless each and every one of you beyond belief and measure.

Kendall is stABLE and God is ABLE.

FORTY-FOUR

THE MARATHON

࿐࿐࿐࿐࿐✝࿐࿐࿐࿐࿐

July 12

Who is Kendall? What happened? When will she talk and walk again? Where is Kendall? How is she doing? Why did this happen? These are just a few of the questions that I get asked on a daily basis. Who knew such a simple question as "How are you?" would be the hardest question of my life to answer; it's such a loaded question, and there is no one-word answer or a simple explanation.

Twenty-six weeks ago, Kendall was completely unconscious and unresponsive. She did not respond to sound, touch, or pain. She was just a stiff, motionless body functioning and surviving off of machines, several medications, and at the Mercy of God. She was neurostorming constantly, which is like an electrical brain thunderstorm—all the brain pathways moving uncontrollably like hot wires.

There I was, standing in the storm, being blinded with unstoppable tears, crying out and thinking that all hope is lost. And all the doctors kept saying was that this is a marathon, not a sprint. Although I began to repeat the same line, it took me several weeks before I truly understood what this meant.

I want to take this time to break down this journey we're on and give you insight into the who, the what, the when, the where, the how, and the why.

Kendall's physical state is very similar to that of a newborn baby in regard to motor function. She has to relearn head control, relearn to sit up supported and unsupported, relearn to stand supported and unsupported, and then eventually relearn to walk. She cannot eat by mouth, talk, or walk. She makes sounds, and like the parents of a newborn, we can tell what each sound means. We know when she's in pain, tired, doesn't want to do something, and when she is just up to her shenanigans. But unlike a newborn baby, Kendall has to learn how to swallow, which includes the speech pathologist or us stimulating her facial muscles. This will start sending signals to the brain to remind it to use those muscles. Once her tongue learns how to move up, down, back, forth, and side to side, then Kendall will be able to eat food by mouth . . . THE MARATHON.

She went through this process with her vision as well in which her eye muscles had to be stimulated. She had to learn how to keep her eyes open, learn how to look up, down, left, right, and past midline (her nose) . . . THE MARATHON.

This process of stimulating the brain will be very similar for her other senses as well—hearing, touching, and smelling . . . THE MARATHON.

To keep it short and simple, every muscle in her body has to be stimulated individually in order for her brain to remember how to use them. Then each function/movement of every muscle has to be relearned (an action that we were taught) or learned (an action that we were naturally born with) . . . THE MARATHON.

Kendall's neurological state—comprehension and memory—is difficult to determine at this time. Although she is alert and responsive, she is not completely conscious until she speaks . . . THE MARATHON.

But what I can tell you is that she is definitely still in there. Her sense of humor is intact, and after weeks of no form of communication, we finally have a way to talk to our baby girl. Using her right hand, she can say "yes," "no," "I love you," "more please" when she wants the food we're eating, and she can show us "Kendall Strong" by flexing her right bicep muscle.

Visually, Kendall can focus on up to eight objects at one time and distinguish between four different words written on the whiteboard before she gets frustrated or confused . . . THE MARATHON.

She knows she is in the hospital due to an accident. She knows the year. She knows her first and last name, and she knows our first names. She can recognize typical objects such as dog, ball, house, and bed. However, she does not understand directional terms such as right and left. She visually cannot process more than two-word commands, such as "close your eyes." But, if we just write, "Close eyes," she can do it . . . THE MARATHON.

Once the speech pathologist and neuropsychologist identify Kendall's current maximum potential, then they will create a communication board. This board will constantly change as Kendall progresses and eventually speaks . . . THE MARATHON.

Kendall is having surgery today to replace her G-tube (feeding tube) with a G-button (mickey). She is also getting cosmetic and phenol injections to help relax those tight muscles and help improve motor function, especially in her right knee and right ankle. Right now, Kendall can purposefully move the entire right side of her body. She can feel sensation on her left and has involuntary movement . . . THE MARATHON.

This entire journey, like life, is a marathon. What may seem like a sprint to some, may be a lifetime for others. Going through this journey with Kendall gives me a whole new meaning and a new appreciation of "Thank you, Lord, for waking me up this morning," because the wake-up for Kendall once was, "Lord, just open one eye today."

Kendall is stABLE and God is ABLE.

FORTY-FIVE

I Need Thee, Oh, I Need Thee

❧❧❧❧❧❧ † ❧❧❧❧❧❧

July 19

For a little over two weeks, I have tried to remain worry-free despite my current situation. Our oldest daughter, Camryn, had COVID with cold-like symptoms. We couldn't risk being around Camryn for obvious reasons, but we could not be without seeing her either. And of course, my mind started getting the best of me with the "what ifs" and the "who is going to."

For four days, we were on eggshells . . . waiting to get tested and finding out the results.

Meanwhile, the stress levels elevated further because our youngest two, Chase and Kaiden, went to Florida. Just knowing they were going to be in a pool daily didn't help either, especially since Chase loves jumping in the water and Kaiden can't swim. All I kept doing was mentally flooding my mind with thoughts of head injuries and near drownings. The recent loss of a mother's four-year-old son, and all of the many other water tragedies so far this summer, didn't help at all. It was the first time in a while that I was worried about all of our children.

Every morning since Kendall's accident, I have played various gospel artist stations on my music app for an hour and have one-on-one time with God. It is a time when I unleash all of my burdens to God. It is a time when I cry the loudest. It is a time when I praise the most. It is a time when I look in the mirror, stripped of everything, and truly "see" me . . . a Black woman, a wife, a mother, a daughter, a sister, a chiropractor, a *soror*, a friend, a Christian, a rusty piano player, life-of-the-party type of girl—but no title could ever compare to that of a praying mother.

On Sunday, my husband and I took Kendall to church service at the CHOA Chapel. The chaplain's message was simple, "You've been invited." God is inviting us to come into His house and cast our burdens, to be a light and to shine our light for others to see.

A mother stood up, and I immediately began to cry because I felt a hurt so deep just from her demeanor. She initially was very soft-spoken because she has never fully disclosed to anyone what she was going through. For the first time, she was vulnerable. She stated that one child had seizures, another child had scoliosis and is currently dealing with vomiting issues, a third child is on the spectrum, and she is currently waiting on results to see if her husband has cancer. This mother has the weight of the world on her shoulders.

She said people, including her job, could not believe she had been dealing with all of this; she just recently asked for time off, and they just found out why. They kept saying, "But you don't look or act like anything is wrong. You still have a smile on your face. How do you keep going?" As she was sharing her journey, she said one thing that touched me and changed my entire outlook. She said effortlessly, "I take it hour by hour. I need God hourly."

There's a familiar hymn that simply says:

I need Thee, Oh, I need Thee.
Every hour I need Thee.
Oh, bless me now, my Savior.
I come to Thee.

This marathon requires strength and endurance, but without God, nothing will be possible. I need God hourly because everything can change, and has changed, in the blink of an eye.

Life is full of the unexpected, and for that reason, God must be the head, Jesus must be your friend, and the Holy Spirit must be within you. That Trinity is what has carried me and will continue to carry me even when my light dims and my hope and faith waver. I need God every hour and if I can inhale, wiggle my fingers and toes, talk, eat, and walk, then my light should be shining bright, because the Kendalls of world need to see it.

So, stop soliciting unspoken prayers and only posting sad emotions. Tell your story. It might just be the light someone else needs. For I am a living witness that triumphs come out of tragedies.

Kendall is dealing with vomiting issues, almost no range of motion in her right ankle, and limited range of motion in her right knee. The physical therapist is doing serial casting to help improve these limitations. This is the last resort or she will have to have another surgery. She is still progressing otherwise with making more sounds, swallowing, and sitting up for 10 seconds unsupported.

Kendall is stABLE and God is ABLE.

FORTY-SIX

THE BEST IS YET TO COME

❀❀❀❀❀❀✝❀❀❀❀❀

July 26

On Saturday, Kendall had a seizure. Yes, it was her first, but I'm refraining from using the word first because it implies that there will be a second, a third . . . So, I simply speak life.

My husband and I had gone to dinner, and upon our return to her room, the nurses at the station stopped us. They asked if Kendall's nurse called us because Kendall had a seizure. Immediately, our hearts sank and that relaxed, carefree moment we were basking in quickly vanished from our faces. We said no and hastily went to Kendall's room; we later realized she *had* called us. All I did was paint the worst type of seizure in my mind, wondering what state Kendall was going to be in. Bad images and thoughts were getting the best of me in just a few short seconds.

When we arrived at Kendall's room, she immediately waved at us, smiling. She was looking like, *What's wrong with y'all*? Her nurse came in and told us her seizure lasted for about a minute. In that minute, the nurse said Kendall's left leg was shaking uncontrollably, her right arm was fully extended, her head was turned to the right, and her eyes were rolled back. We made light of the situation by telling Kendall she didn't have to have a seizure if all she wanted was for us to stay with her and not eat. Kendall smiled, and we all laughed.

As soon as the nurse left, our smiling, laughing faces faded instantly, and my husband and I just stared at Kendall in silence.

What he was starting to display on the outside was what I was feeling on the inside. We weren't there. We weren't there when she had her accident, and now once again, we weren't there when she had a seizure. Just as soon as we'd finally learned to escape that dark, cold, and lonely place, this news took us back to what had become a comfortable place of heartache and depression. Crying motionless in the shower had once again become a daily routine.

From the highest of highs to the lowest of lows, Kendall's accident, our journey, has been a miracle slowly unfolding before our eyes. With all of the initial setbacks came many disappointments, heartaches, and a spirit of discouragement. There were moments of not eating or sleeping, moments of despair and desperation, moments of anger and anxiety, moments of helplessness and hopelessness, moments . . . unshakable moments . . . unbearable moments. I found myself struggling, and still do, with the weight I'm carrying, and I wonder how much God really thinks I can bear.

What happens when the strong get weak? What happens when the silence is too loud? What happens when the weight is too much?

I found myself crying frantically out to God, "That's too much! That's too much!" But the more I cried out, the more weight was added. The more I prayed, the more weight was added. The more I praised, the more weight was added. I felt defeated. I couldn't win. I couldn't catch a break.

Although I was on this emotional roller coaster and fighting what seemed like a losing battle, there was one thing that was consistent—God never left me. After every single cry, prayer, and praise, God whispered sweetly in my ear, "The best is yet to come. Keep pushing."

This accident is an unimaginable tragedy. It turned two families' worlds upside down and forever stained our hearts. It mentally affected several people who witnessed Kendall's accident. It emotionally affected a multitude of people who were genuinely afflicted. But out of this tragedy came triumphs. The unbelievers now believe. People started praying more. People's faith increased. People were coming back to God.

This journey has erased color barriers. It has erased religious barriers. It has erased cultural barriers. It has erased socioeconomic barriers. It has erased ocean barriers. This journey has been about the power of God, the love of community, and the miracle for Kendall.

This isn't my story. This isn't Kendall's story. This is our story, and THE BEST IS YET TO COME.

Kendall is doing well. The neurologist will get an EEG (a recording of brain activity), put her on seizure medications for three months, and then reevaluate her. Kendall is making great progress despite the seizure. God is real, prayer works, and Kendall is truly a living testimony.

Kendall is stABLE and God is ABLE.

FORTY-SEVEN

LET IT SHINE

᳀᳀᳀᳀᳀ † ᳀᳀᳀᳀᳀

August 2

Open House was very difficult for me. I was once again slipping away into that dark place because we have approached another "first" without Kendall.

Not only was Kendall not present but just hearing the word "school" and phrases like "be safe" and seeing crosswalks, school buses, and the sign, "#PRAYFORKENDALL #TEAMTHOMAS," located near her accident scene, took me right back to January 11, 2022. Tears slowly filled my eyes with every step as we walked through elementary, middle, and high school hallways.

The looks of sympathy, empathy, and "fame" were piercing, and the hugs of comfort and excitement were unsettling. My head was spinning, my heart was pounding, and my limbs were quivering. The more people we encountered, the more I was looking for an escape. I was trapped in a sea of unwavering love and support that was merely suffocating my soul.

I simply wanted Open House to focus on Kaiden, Chase, and Camryn. I wanted them to just have one moment to themselves. I wanted one moment to not dwell on Kendall's current situation. We *needed* that moment.

Yesterday was the first day of school. It is usually an exciting day for all the parents and some children. It is a day I vowed to never work since Camryn's kindergarten mix-up (a story for another day). It is the day I take my infamous individual and group photos of the children, and I even cook breakfast. I would see them off to school with a hug and my lecture: "Focus, listen, and behave. I love you." Then, I would relax, binge-watch some shows, and wait for the children to return home safely from school. And as usual, one of the four would have a great day and the other three would be like, *School was boring*. In my true mama fashion, I would say, "It was boring because y'all are boring; you should be having the time of your life at school because being an adult sucks." We all would laugh as the children began to mock me with all my crazy sayings.

But there was nothing *usual* about *this* first day of school. Kendall wasn't there. My husband and I weren't home to see the children because we stay at the hospital with Kendall. I couldn't take my infamous photos, and I couldn't cook breakfast. I didn't have to request off from work because I haven't been able to work since Kendall's accident. There were no hugs to give and no seeing them off to school. There was no relaxing or binge-watching. There was only a sense of emptiness accompanied with guilt, anguish, and despair. My darkness was overshadowing my light.

Just as I was about to succumb to the darkness, I reflected on this past Sunday's sermon given by my executive pastor. He simply stated, "Go get your shine." Just as the sun begins to rise, the darkness will soon fade away. Eventually, the Son, the Light, will overshadow the darkness.

January 11, 2022, was very dark and there have been (and will be) other dark moments during this journey. Eventually, the progress, the light, will shine so bright that the darkness will just be lost in the transition. In these moments, I'm reminded of a simple gospel song that says:

> *This little light of mine,*
> *I'm gonna let it shine.*
> *This little light of mine,*
> *I'm gonna let it shine.*
> *This little light of mine,*

I'm gonna let it shine.
Let it shine, let it shine, oh let it shine.

Kendall is progressing well. Her initial three-day stay in inpatient rehabilitation has been extended another three weeks. The more she progresses, the longer her stay. As much as we all want Kendall to come home, I pray she keeps getting extensions. She is continuing to swallow more including purees, juices, ice chips, popsicles, pudding, yogurt, and mashed potatoes. She is starting to communicate not only with some hand and head gestures but with some pen-to-paper writing and writing using a touchscreen tablet. She is becoming more vocal by making more sounds. She is getting stronger on her right side, and her left side is starting to show minute voluntary movement.

Kendall is stABLE and God is ABLE.

FORTY-EIGHT

You Know My Name

☙☙☙☙☙†☙☙☙☙☙

August 9

For 30 weeks, I have watched and waited for any sign that Kendall was going to be all right. For 30 weeks, I have been masquerading my darkest moments and suppressing my deepest thoughts. Every day, for 30 weeks, I wake up as if I'm preparing myself for a dress rehearsal for this big production of a tragedy, only to realize later that *this production* is my reality.

Am I living someone else's life? Because *this* can't possibly be mine. Am I having an out-of-body experience?

For 30 weeks, I have cried tears of frustration, tears of confusion, tears of disappointment, tears of hopelessness, tears of defeat. And just when I think I'm all cried out, God steps in and those tears became tears of joy, tears of assurance, tears of triumph, tears of euphoria, tears of victory.

According to "Rancho Los Amigos Levels of Cognitive Functioning Scale: A Guide for Family and Friends," there are eight levels of consciousness, and for pediatric traumatic brain injuries, the levels are divided by the following:

- **Level I: No response.** The patient does not respond to any stimulus and is in a deep sleep.
- **Level II: Generalized response.** The patient sleeps most of the time and may respond to stimulus.
- **Level III: Localized response.** The patient is awake

longer during the day and will respond to stimulus by moving a limb.

- **Level IV: Confused–Agitated.** The injured brain is starting to improve and wake up. However, the patient struggles to control his or her response to the environment. The patient is very agitated and cries and screams even after the stimulus has been removed. The patient struggles with memory and is very confused. Some patients become violent, and their memories will only be what happened before the accident. This level is the scariest.
- **Level V: Confused–Inappropriate–Non-agitated.** The patient is more awake. The patient can follow commands after being instructed several times. The patient cannot focus for long. The patient may display inappropriate behavior such as poor manners or making sexual comments.
- **Level VI: Confused–Appropriate.** The patient will still be confused and struggle with memories since his or her accident. Learning will be difficult. Everything becomes routine. Some patients may act selfish.
- **Level VII: Automatic–Appropriate.** The patient does daily routines with little confusion. He or she can learn new things but at a slower pace than before due to the brain injury. However, the patient has poor judgment skills and cannot be left alone.
- **Level VIII: Purposeful–Appropriate.** The patient's memory has improved and his or her behavior is appropriate. Only close family and friends will pick up on any problems with thinking or behavior. The patient can function in most social environments.

This past week has been one of the hardest weeks to watch Kendall. Kendall is usually a willing participant with her daily therapies—unless she's up to her shenanigans, as I call it. This is when she plays sleep or pretends to moan in pain to avoid doing her therapy. As soon as I say, "Kendall, I'm not having your shenanigans today," she turns her head to me and smiles showing her teeth.

But last week was different. Kendall was moaning, crying (still without tears), and screaming as if she was being harmed. Even when the staff or my husband and I stopped with her therapies or put her in her bed or in her chair, or were quiet, she was still very vocal. Nothing and no one could soothe her. She was so disturbed and distressed. I couldn't bear to watch her like that any longer. This went on for a few days and then it dawned on me—Kendall is waking up more and is transitioning to a Level IV: Confused–Agitated on the Rancho Scale.

Through this difficult level of consciousness, Kendall still amazes me daily with her progression. Last Wednesday, Kendall was attempting to speak. She started screaming, her lips began to quiver, and she was shaking her head from side to side. Just as we were trying to comfort and soothe her, she did the unexpected. She squealed out the word "mom." And following that same pattern of screaming, quivering lips, and head shaking after every syllable, she blurted out the words "dad" and "bye." We were speechless and in awe of God's miracle and answered prayers unfolding before our eyes. Our baby girl, our Kendall, *spoke*!

For 30 weeks, we have not heard Kendall say a word. For 30 weeks, we have anticipated the day that Kendall would speak. From last Wednesday until Saturday, Kendall had been saying one- to two-syllable words accompanied with the screaming, quivering lips, and head shaking.

Every day, we start off with praise and worship for an hour, listening to Speak to My Heart on a music app. Kendall and I will do dance movements with our hands as I sing to her. On Sunday, Kendall and I were listening to a song entitled, "You Know My Name" by Tasha Cobbs Leonard. The words simply say:

He knows my name.
Yes, he knows my name.
He knows my name.
Yes, he knows my name.
And oh, how he walks with me.
Yes oh, how he talks with me.
And oh, how he tells me,
That I am his own.
You know my name.
You know my name.
You know my name.
You know my name.

But this time, Kendall kept pointing at me when I would sing the line, "You know my name." Finally, I asked her, "Do you know my name?" She smiled and gave me a thumbs-up. She screamed a little, her lips quivered, and her head swayed from side to side. Then, ever so shockingly, she said, "Shah . . . nah." She did the same thing to her dad and said, "Kel . . . vin."

Tears flowed from my face and all I could say was, "Kendall knows my name. Kendall knows my name. You know my name."

Thank you, God! HE knows my name!

Kendall is stABLE and God is ABLE.

FORTY-NINE

IT'S **GOLDEN**

❧❧❧❧❧✝❧❧❧❧❧

August 16

Martin Luther King Jr. Day. Valentine's Day. Kaiden's eighth birthday. My husband's birthday. Easter. Camryn's Sweet 16 birthday. Mother's Day. My birthday. Father's Day. Chase's 12th birthday. The first day of school . . . These were the celebrations and holidays that we had to manage without Kendall in the midst.

We were so out of touch at times that when asked how many, my husband and Chase would cheerfully say seven! We're a party of seven! Dreadfully, I would say, it's just six of us; Kendall is not here. Then the atmosphere would shift like the wave moving slowly at a football game as I glanced at everyone's face. Suddenly, our happiness turned into sorrow. And like a broken record, on every occasion, we would ride this emotional roller coaster of highs and lows trying to make the best of our circumstances.

But this next celebration was going to be different. I mean, it *must* be different, because this time, it's Kendall's birthday. It's the one celebration that we shouldn't possibly have to figure out how to cope without her.

It was Kendall's golden birthday. She was turning 15 on the 15th. For the months leading up to her birthday, everyone had been brainstorming as to how we should celebrate. *This birthday* had to be epic, because January 11, 2022, could have easily been her sunset date. But God . . . God had other plans. He was not and is not through with Kendall.

Kendall had a three-day golden birthday celebration that kicked off on Saturday, August 13, 2022. She was showered with gifts and serenaded by the Sling Queenz, Atlanta Slingshot Community, and Savage Ryders. They rode from Douglasville, Georgia, to Children's Healthcare of Atlanta at Scottish Rite in Atlanta, Georgia. Their presence was a pure delight, not only for Kendall but for the other children as well as the staff. Tears of joy flowed as my husband and I watched Kendall, with the sun shining ever so gently across her face, in a euphoric state as the riders drove by. I could only imagine how this must feel like paradise to her.

Sunday, August 14, 2022, was all about quality time with the family. She was surrounded by her grandmother, two sisters, and her brother who brought pure joy and cheerfulness. They were all over her—laughing, sharing stories, and traveling down memory lane.

Then the moment had finally arrived—Monday, August 15, 2022, Kendall's golden birthday! My husband and I were decked out in our bright red T-shirts with the #KENDALLSTRONG43 logo in white ink across our chests. Kendall had a custom-made black T-shirt that said, "It's my GOLDEN Birthday, 15 on the 15th. Of course, the lettering was sparkling gold and white.

During motivational Monday, we sang happy birthday to Kendall and shared Kendall's birthday cake with the children and staff. It was a pull-apart cake in the shape of a football jersey with pink and yellow trimming; it had Kendall's name in the center and the number 15 under it. A cake fit perfectly for a princess warrior who happens to play football.

Throughout the day and between therapies, we partied, ate cake and ice cream, and gave out goodie bags filled with lollipops, bubbles, and #KendallStrong43 bracelets.

This birthday was truly golden. Honestly, I had never heard of a *golden* birthday until last week. Everyone kept saying it, and I would just go with the flow. Finally, someone said, "She'll be 15 on the 15th. That's golden! Golden . . . Golden . . . Golden.

Golden means something is wonderful because it is likely to be successful and rewarding, or because it is the best of its kind. When something is *GO*l*D*en, it means favorable and prosperous. There is nothing *GO*l*D*en without God. Kendall is a true testament to God's favor, and she is walking in prosperity.

Life is good, but the breath of life is *GO*l*D*en.

Kendall is stABLE and God is ABLE.

FIFTY

Unexpecting the Unexpected

༖༖༖༖༖✝༙༙༙༙༙

August 17

For almost a week, my husband and I were made aware that Kendall would be getting discharged on August 17, 2022, just two days after her golden birthday. I decided we should keep quiet and surprise everyone. Last time, when we were at Children's Healthcare of Atlanta at Scottish Rite, Kendall was given five different discharge dates. My mother and our children would get so excited and then crushed when the date kept changing. After the third date change, I couldn't bear to see the disappointment in their faces again.

I had it all planned out this time around. By the time we would arrive home, Kaiden, Chase, and Camryn would be home from school; my mother would be out at Marietta Fish Market for an early dinner with her friend. She would come home to a wonderful surprise.

Wednesday was a perfect day because it was one of the few days where there were no after-school activities, and Camryn did not have to go to work. What could possibly go wrong?

Discharge day at the hospital is an all-day event. Although Kendall does not have any therapies, it is a day of checks and balances, group pictures, and heartfelt "see you laters." It is a day of trying to figure out how we accumulated so much stuff again while at the same time acquiring huge care packages from the hospital staff. It is a day of reflecting on how far Kendall has progressed this time around. It is a day of exchanging numbers with strangers that became sources of comfort in this unexpected club. It is the day that Team Thomas was going to be a party of seven again!

On the ride home, Kendall was so agitated and looked very uncomfortable in her chair. As much as she was ready to come home, there wasn't a smile anywhere in sight. Meanwhile, we were entangled in the worst traffic that extended our typical trip time of 50 minutes to one hour and 30 minutes. I was also trying to process the two separate emails I'd just received regarding Chase's behavior in music appreciation and math. On top of all of that, my mother called stating she had to cancel plans with her friend because Kaiden, our eight-year-old daughter, was not feeling well. She said Kaiden came home with a headache and a fever, and that Camryn, our 16-year-old daughter, was getting ready to test Kaiden for COVID. Before I could get a word in, she said she'd call me back.

At this point, I had no other choice but to call my mother back and tell her the exciting news. As soon as she answered the phone, she said, "Kaiden has COVID. Don't come until Monday." Then she said, "Let me call you back."

I hung up with a pit in the bottom of my stomach, and my mind started wandering as my heart beat a little faster. We can't go back to the hospital. We can't get a hotel room because Kendall must sleep in a hospital bed. The "we can't do this because of that" was getting the best of me. I was going down the rabbit hole.

I looked at my husband with disenchantment. He said, "Tell her." I called my mother back, interrupting her calls of informing those who had been in close contact with Kaiden. Softly and slowly, I said, "Well, we're on our way home . . . with Kendall." My mother was still her jovial self, full of excitement, despite our current situation.

The homecoming I'd foreseen was not the one Kendall received. Kendall was irritable. Kaiden had COVID. Chase was hesitant around us because he knew we received emails from his teachers. Camryn was exhausted. My husband was aggravated, and I was in a state of disbelief. The loudness of the entire house became mute as I surveyed the chaos around me, the accumulation of three months of hospital stays, the contents of medical supply boxes scattered about, the remnants of school activities, a melancholy atmosphere, and the uncertainty of life.

I stood in the shower that night and wept, saying, "My God, how much do you think I can bear?" God said as much as He can carry me through.

Kendall is stABLE and God is ABLE.

FIFTY-ONE

Patience Is a Virtue

August 23

We have been home for one day shy of a week now. I'm restless. I'm moody. And my tolerance level is at an all-time low. Summer has almost passed us by.

We had been living off of hospital food, which was either a blessing in disguise or a toilet-trip surprise. Hence, we ate out a lot. We slept on makeshift beds and pull-out couches that made bus seats feel like feather-top mattresses. The temperature was always cold which complemented our lukewarm, low-pressure shower. To top it all off, I, personally, was playing human dodgeball with service dogs at CHOA. It seems like everywhere I turned, there was a dog. (Side note: I'm terrified of all dogs, any size, any kind.) And just when we could finally get some sleep, we would be awakened to the sounds of random code reds, blues, and purples. So we were looking forward to coming home because this was our life—two different hospitals, consecutively, from May 18 to August 17.

> HOME, SWEET HOME.
> HOME, IT'S NOT A PLACE . . . IT'S A FEELING.
> HOME IS MY HAPPY PLACE.
> BLESS THIS HOUSE.

These were all the signs staring at me as I entered our home, but home didn't feel so sweet. Home definitely had me feeling some type of way. Home wasn't so happy; it was chaotic. And "Bless this house" took on the same connotation as someone saying, "Bless your heart" —and not the good meaning either.

At the hospital, feeding her, administering her medications, and bathing her were optional. Our only job was getting her ready in the mornings and getting her to therapy.

My husband and I quickly forgot how physically taxing and mentally draining it is to care for Kendall. She is still 100% dependent on us for all her needs, and we still do not have any additional help at home. No nurse. No care partner or tech.

Our day starts at 6:00 a.m. and ends around 10:00 p.m., if we're fortunate. During this time, we bathe her, change her diapers, administer her medications, and gravity-feed her through her G-button (a.k.a. mickey). We are also taking her to and from appointments as well as doing our own version of speech, occupational, and physical therapy until she starts outpatient rehabilitation.

In the midst of it all, we have to get Chase to football practice, Camryn to work, cater to Kaiden's quarantine needs, and do whatever else is required of us as parents.

Just like a newborn, Kendall gets irritated throughout the night. Her favorite fuss time is 3:36 a.m. By the time we figure out what's wrong and get her calm, it's in the 4 o'clock hour; then, boom, my 5:50 a.m. alarm is going off. And everyone says, "Make sure y'all take time for yourselves." Who? When? How? Where? I just want to sleep, get my back rubbed, and indulge in some adult beverages on a beach somewhere.

But in the midnight hour, when Kendall is at peace with her eyes closed and the house is quiet, I have a moment of tranquility. Home becomes a sweet feeling. It becomes a happy place. And I whisper to God to bless this house. And God whispers back, "Patience is a virtue."

Patience . . . Patience . . . Patience. It is the ability to endure difficult circumstances without complaining. It is a quality of self-restraint and is compared to God's mercy and compassion. Patience is what I need. Patience is what will get me through this marathon. Patience is my destiny.

Kendall is stABLE and God is ABLE.

FIFTY-TWO

THERE'S A MIRACLE IN THIS ROOM

ॐॐॐॐॐ✝ॐॐॐॐॐ

August 30

Our second week home was much better than the first. My mother, without hesitation, washed her hands free of being in charge, and we reestablished order with the other three children. We deprogrammed them from their "but grandma does this and grandma said that." When will they learn that I'm not grandma? She's sweet, and I'm not with their antics—or as I like to say, their shenanigans.

All of Kendall's care packages that had accumulated since January were finally assorted and have a place to call home. We stopped living out of our suitcases and unpacked them. My husband started his home projects, and I quickly resumed the role of "go ask your mother." Kendall was slowly but surely finding her happy place and was definitely less agitated; my husband and I could actually sleep in our bed a little more peacefully.

Now that we're all settled in, we invited some close family and friends to visit Kendall. Everyone has been so patient and considerate during this entire incident. Their prayers and generosity have truly blessed us in so many ways, known and unknown. So, it is only befitting that we open our doors and let them see what answered prayers look like. Their emotions ran high as they all looked in awe of Kendall. They were speechless. Kendall wasn't

116

supposed to be here, but God saw differently. All they could say was, "There's a miracle in this room." Kendall is a miracle—a living testimony.

A miracle. A miracle. "A miracle" is all I have been hearing off and on since January 11, 2022. God's going to use His miraculous power to save Kendall. She is a miracle. There's a miracle coming your way. But what did all that mean? A miracle is an extraordinary event that is not due to something natural or any scientific laws; it is "the work of a divine agency," according to *Oxford Languages.*

Kendall's accident was a near-fatality. She was in the neuro ICU for a little over two months—a floor in which *most* don't survive. She couldn't open her eyes; she couldn't open her mouth to eat; she couldn't talk; she couldn't walk. She was just a body surviving off electrical stimulation and oxygen from all kinds of medical devices.

But God began to break every chain and the miracles started to unfold. His supernatural powers began to shine. Kendall survived her near-fatal accident. She left that neuro ICU floor and went to a rehabilitation facility. She opened her eyes; she opened her mouth; she is starting to talk; and one day, she *will* walk.

That divine agency is nobody but God. He's a wonder, a marvelous wonder. There's a miracle in this room. There's a miracle in this house. And it's got Kendall's name all over it!

Kendall is stABLE and God is ABLE.

Acknowledgments

If I had ten thousand tongues, it wouldn't be enough to say thank you for the many blessings. It wouldn't be enough to say thank you for your continuous prayers. It wouldn't be enough to say thank you, God.

I am forever in debt to my mother, Evelyn Dunham. She has been my rock and my tangible source of strength, not only during this unimaginable accident but throughout my life. She is a phenomenal woman and a beautiful soul inside and out. I have always admired her resilience and her ability to withstand the storms of life. Her love, affection, dedication, and compassion toward others speak volumes. Thank you for taking care of Camryn, Chase, and Kaiden while Kelvin and I were at the hospital with Kendall. Thank you for being the GOAT of grandmas! I love you for eternity, and I simply thank you from the bottom of my heart.

To my husband, Kelvin Thomas. This journey could have destroyed us. It could have taken us to a point of no return but instead, it transformed us as a couple, as parents, as lovers, and as friends. When I needed to be held, you were there. When I needed to be comforted, you were there. When I needed to scream, cry, or yell, you were there. I truly appreciate you being there with me in the midnight hour, wiping my tears as I was writing this book. You were always there, and for that, I love you the most and always. I am forever thankful for your unconditional and never-ending love.

My children are my world. They are the epicenter of my heart. Their inner strength and mental endurance have been nothing short of a miracle during this horrific transition.

Camryn Sierra, you surprise me. Kendall's accident could have mentally set you back into that dark place. Instead, you kept your head up and mustered up enough energy to press forward. I am so proud of you. Thank you for being so courageous.

Kendall Elise, this book wouldn't even be possible without you. This is your story. I thank you for allowing me to simply be an instrument. It is your fighting spirit that kept me going. It is your ability to think outside of the box that kept pushing me. It is your willingness to live that kept me from drowning. Thank you for helping unfold this gift of writing that I never knew was in me.

Chase Khalil, you amaze me. My heart sank when I discovered you witnessed Kendall's accident. You were so vulnerable and fragile, but God shielded your mind and protected your heart. You came out on the other side with more buoyancy. Thank you for being so brave.

Kaiden Sanaa, you soothe me. Kaiden, you were the first person to inform me of Kendall's accident. Although you were seven years old at the time, you had a way of holding back your anxiety while simultaneously protecting me from my worst fears. Kaiden always comforted me and wiped my never-ending tears. Kaiden has definitely been here before and has a wonderful old soul within her. Thank you for being true to yourself. Thank you for your bubbly personality and your tenacity.

Camryn, Kendall, Chase, and Kaiden, thank you for making me a better parent. I love you all beyond infinity.

To my other family members, near and far. I love you all from the depths of my soul. Thank you for prayers, calls, texts, and surprise visits. Thank you for taking time out of your busy days and checking on us. Thank you for your unfaltering love.

Rev. Dr. Taruway Richard Allen Bright Sr. is the senior pastor of my church, Turner Chapel AME. Over the past few years, Rev. Bright has become more than a pastor; he is family. Rev. Bright is a testament to the awesomeness of God. His faith is unwavering, and his love for God, his church, his neighbor, and his sisters and brothers in Christ are remarkable. When I broke the news to Rev. Bright regarding Kendall's accident, his heart dropped. He was immensely distraught as if it were his own daughter. All he kept saying was, "This is personal. This is personal." It was at that moment I knew Rev. Bright was going to do everything in his power to get us through this mountain, even if he had to move the mountain himself. I am grateful for the unlimited access we had to him. I am grateful for his powerful prayers. I am grateful for the extraordinary support, not only from Rev. Bright but from my entire Turner Chapel family.

A very special thanks to Rev. Don Ezell, Rev. Cassandra Marcus, Rev. Lynn Burkhead, and Mother Bertha Fordham.

Monica South, Shamella Gaillard, and Jamie Grice-Grinage are three amazing ladies that have carried me through, what I thought then, were some pretty tough times in my life. We have been each other's sounding board, a shoulder to cry on, and a phone call away. Although there were a few other close women in my life who have also been there, these three ladies put their lives on hold just to physically be with me during this difficult transition. Monica, you are my bestie and there is nothing that will break our bond. Shamella, you are my golden girl and there is no distance that will keep us apart. Jamie, you are my ally and there is nothing that will divide us. Thank you, ladies, for being more than a friend; thank you for being my sisters. I love you all until the end of time.

To Littie Brown, I will never forget the day that you put an APB out on me, searching for my number. Who knew that the message from Rev. Bright to call you would be a life-changing event. Thank you for not only believing in me but for being the financial resource behind this book project. I thank you for listening to God and allowing Him to use you as a vessel to help me with this book. You are truly a Godsend. Thank you from the bottom of my heart.

To Wanda Cohen Clark, I never knew I was a writer until our paths crossed. I never knew that with your expertise as an editor, this book would change so many lives. I am so honored to have had the pleasure of working closely with you on my book project. I am looking forward to what this relationship will blossom into. The sky is the limit. Thank you for finding time to guide me and pour your heart and soul into this project. I am forever thankful for you.

Angela Johnson, you have been through the fire and back with my family. You have counseled us through some trials and tribulations. When Kendall's accident happened, I knew I could count on you to provide that mental support and stability we desperately needed. Thank you for being that sounding board and that shoulder to cry on. Thank you for keeping us together as a family unit and praying for us. We all need Jesus and a great therapist; fortunate for us, we had both!

Kendall was initially taken to Wellstar Kennestone Hospital in Marietta, Georgia. It was there in which she was blessed with the best neurosurgeon. He genuinely seeks the best possible outcome for his patients, and he has an impeccable bedside manner. He is Heaven-sent. His hands are blessed, and his heart is pure. His experience and dedication to his patients go above his call of duty. I am beyond thankful for the neurosurgeon and his entire team, and the critical care team, Dr. Eli Feen, Dr. Campbell, and Dr. Ragland.

A special thanks to the entire staff at Kennestone Hospital—custodians, care partners, social workers, nurses, doctors, cafeteria, the Bistro, parking-lot attendants, volunteers, security, and any other employees whose paths crossed ours.

Kendall was completely unconscious when she was transferred to CHOA. Their Comprehensive Inpatient Rehabilitation Unit (CIRU) was outstanding. Under the dynamic guidance of Dr. Poplawski, Dr. Vova, and Dr. Jones, Kendall was able to defy the odds. Kendall had extraordinary therapists as well that pushed her onto the road to greatness.

I am also overwhelmed with gratitude for Dr. Howarth, Emily, Amber, Andrea, Tori, Lori, Cori, and Shayna.

A special thanks to Mrs. Annie Verghese for being that breakthrough that Kendall needed.

I would be remiss if I didn't extend sincere gratitude to the custodians, techs, aides, nurses, doctors, cafeteria staff, security, parking-lot attendants, teachers, therapists, and any other employees and CIRU families.

I would like to thank my alma mater, South Carolina State University, and all the Divine 9 members.

A special thanks to my line sisters and our illustrious sorority, Delta Sigma Theta Sorority, Inc. Thank you for your generosity. Thank you for your continued support and prayers. Thank you for opening your hearts and showing compassion for my family. Your acts of kindness will never be forgotten. Much love and blessings to you all.

I would like to thank the entire chiropractic franchise, The Joint Chiropractic. Thank you for your prayers and support during this difficult time. A special thanks to The Joint Chiropractic in Marietta, Georgia, and to all my coworkers who constantly checked on me and prayed for me. Thank you for your care packages and well wishes. I love you all.

My gratitude also goes out to North Paulding High School, especially the 2021–2022 freshman football team as well as the North Paulding High School Fellowship of Christian Athletes (FCA). This group of young people displayed so much love toward Kendall. They cried and prayed with us. They said words of encouragement, and at every game, a 43-second moment of silence was held in honor of Kendall.

A special thanks to other schools in the area that offered their sincerest empathy: Hiram High School, Hillgrove High School, Sammie McClure Middle School, Burnt Hickory Elementary School, and Shelton Elementary School. I would like to thank all other schools in Paulding and the surrounding counties as well. Your actions did not go unnoticed. I am truly thankful.

I would like to personally extend my gratitude to the Atlanta Falcons, Freddie the Falcon, and the Atlanta Phoenix Women's Football Team for sending Kendall the ultimate football fan swag gear and sharing her love for the sport.

A huge thank you to the Sling Queenz, Atlanta Slingshot Community, Savage Ryders, ATL Slingshot Store, and Uniquely Yours for providing Kendall with an unforgettable golden birthday celebration.

Thank you, Mr. Robert and Mrs. Judy Jenkins, for spearheading Kendall Day, and Rev. Michael A. Smith and your entire congregation of Mount Olive Baptist Church of Acworth, Georgia, for hosting the event and for your continuous prayers and support.

To my Harmony Hills Community, I appreciate each one of you for your contributions.

To Akida "AK" Adisa. I thank you for creating and making #KendallStrong43 T-shirts.

I would also like to thank C. Nicole Henderson, Yameka Wright, and Avery Woodward, an NPHS Class of 2022 graduate, for setting up two separate fundraising accounts for Kendall.

To the 62 Foundation, Team Luke Hope for Minds, and Neighborhood Access Partner, a warm thank-you for all you have provided for Kendall. Thank you for making life a little easier and less stressful during this unimaginable accident. It is people like you all who make difficult times less worrisome. Thank you for just being there and lifting some of our financial burdens. May God continue to bless your foundations tremendously.

During this entire journey, there was one group of individuals that covered me and encouraged me the most. These were the mothers who lost their children to fatal accidents, cancer, and other diseases. They have a strength like no other, and they prayed hard that I would not be a member of their club. For the life of me, I couldn't process it at first. Then Kim Torres, a young mother from Philadelphia, wrote me and shared her testimony. She said her son is in a better place and is at peace; therefore, she is at peace. I could almost feel her joyful spirit as I was reading her letter. To Kim Torres, Liz Honan, and all the parents who have lost, I thank you for uplifting me and praying nonstop for Kendall. May God continue to be your Comforter, Healer, and Peacemaker. Love and blessings to you all.

Our biggest financial and spiritual support came from the kindness of strangers. These are people in the community, across the nation, and overseas. Most of them didn't know Kendall, my family, or had any connection to North Paulding High School. But what they had in common was a giving spirit and a benevolent heart. Kendall's story did not just affect my family, it affected the world. It was the prayers heard around the world that kept Kendall fighting. It was the prayers heard around the world that sustained my family and me. It was the prayers heard around the world that broke every chain and moved mountains. I am so thankful for your monetary gifts, gift cards, care packages, letters, free services (house cleaning, food, haircuts, yard signs, flowers, oil changes, and landscaping), and all other acts of love and kindness we have received. Thank you for being strangers who became our prayer warrior family.

This journey is not just Kendall's or Team Thomas's journey. It's ours. It's a story of how we are overcoming the aftermath of this unimaginable near-fatality. I wholeheartedly thank anyone who has been a part of this story. If you whispered a prayer, I thank you. If you hugged me, I thank you. If you saw me from a distance, I thank you. If you did anything for my family, I thank you. If you thought about Kendall, I thank you. If you purchased a #KendallStrong43 T-shirt, I thank you. If you paid for my household purchases, I thank you. If you shared Kendall's story, I thank you. If you held a fundraiser for Kendall, I thank you. If you shed any tears, I thank you. If you are reading this book, I thank you. If you began praying again, increased your faith, or turned back to God, then God is pleased, and I found my *why* for this journey. And for that, I am forever thankful.

About The Author

SHANNA MCCOLLUM THOMAS served as the clinic director for The Joint Chiropractic in Marietta, Georgia. She is a graduate of South Carolina State University and Life University. She holds a bachelor of science degree in biology and a doctor of chiropractic degree.

She has been practicing chiropractic for almost 17 years. Her career started in Bronx, New York, as an associate chiropractor in personal injury clinics. Four years later, she relocated back to Atlanta, Georgia, and continued practicing in personal injury clinics, wellness clinics, and later started her own mobile chiropractic. Shanna is very passionate and connects with her patients in a way that is unforgettable and irreplaceable.

Born and raised in Brunswick, Georgia, Shanna married her high school sweetheart, Kelvin, on December 24, 2007. They have four beautiful children—three daughters and one son—as well as two aquatic turtles.

Shanna is a member of Turner Chapel AME Church in Marietta, Georgia. She is also a member of Delta Sigma Theta Sorority, Inc.

The Thomases currently reside in Acworth, Georgia.